ST KILDA
The Continuing Story of the Islands

Edited by
Meg Buchanan

GLASGOW
MUSEUMS

EDINBURGH : HMSO

© Glasgow Museums 1995

First published 1995

British Library Cataloguing in Publication Data

A catalogue record for this book is available from the British Library

Exhibition: St Kilda Explored

Art Gallery and Museum, Kelvingrove, Glasgow

20 October 1995 – 25 August 1996

Supported by Scottish Natural Heritage

ISBN 0 11 495172 1

St Kilda

Contents

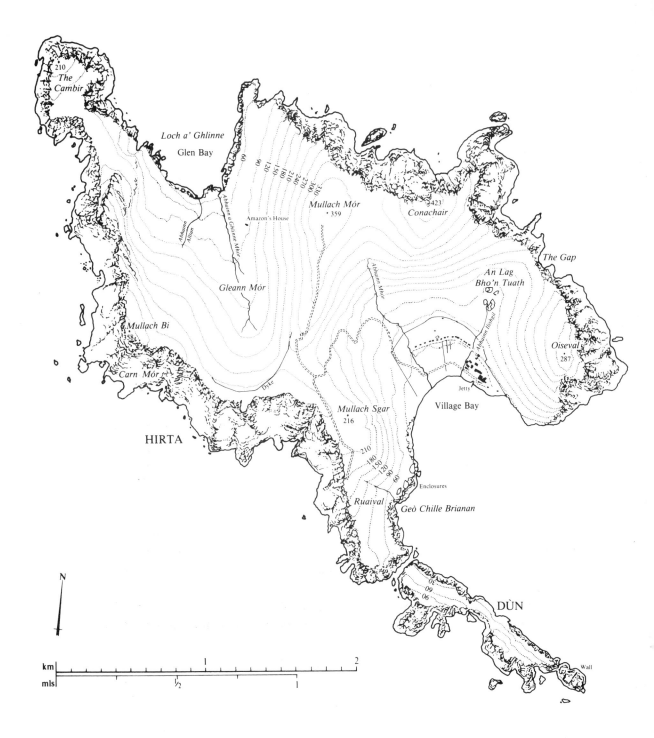

Hirta and Dùn: physical features and outlying structures.

The Authors

MEG BUCHANAN is a curator in the History Department of Glasgow Museums. Since 1976 she has been responsible for the St Kilda collection at the Art Gallery and Museum, Kelvingrove (including since 1989 The National Trust for Scotland loan). In 1980, in commemoration of the 50th anniversary of the evacuation, she produced the exhibition *St Kilda Past and Present* in the St Enoch Exhibition Centre, Glasgow. Publications include: *St Kilda: A Photographic Album.*

MARY HARMAN After an initial trip to St Kilda with a National Trust for Scotland work party in 1974, Mary Harman has visited the islands many times, being involved with building surveys and excavations. She has researched the documentary history of the islands at the University of Edinburgh. She now works in South Uist.

GEOFFREY STELL has been Head of Architecture at The Royal Commission on the Ancient and Historical Monuments of Scotland since 1991. He studied at Leeds and Glasgow Universities before joining RCAHMS in 1969 as an Historic Buildings Investigator. Among other activities, he was founder-Secretary and later served as Chairman of the Scottish Vernacular Buildings Working Group. His publications include, as co-author, *Buildings of St Kilda* and, as co-editor, *Materials and Traditions in Scottish Building.*

NORMAN EMERY graduated from Durham University in Archaeology and in Economic History. He was involved in archaeological excavations and surveys in Northern England and Scotland, particularly Orkney and Shetland, before undertaking work on St Kilda for The National Trust for Scotland. He is now archaeologist for Durham Cathedral.

ALEX MORRISON is Senior Lecturer in the Department of Archaeology, University of Glasgow. His main research interests are the archaeology and environment of early hunter-gatherer societies; rural settlement and cultural landscapes of late and post medieval Scotland. Publications include *Early Man in Britain and Ireland*. He is Editor of the *Glasgow Archaeological Journal* and Vice-President of the Glasgow Archaeological Society.

MARK TASKER is Head of the Seabirds and Cetaceans Branch of the UK Joint Nature Conservation Committee. He is responsible for providing conservation advice on the offshore marine environment and the animals that use those areas. He has been working on seabirds, both on land and at sea, since 1979.

PETER JEWELL is an Emeritus Professor in the Department of Zoology, University of Cambridge. His research has been on the reproduction and ecology of mammals in Britain and Africa. He was one of the group of scientists who initiated the research on the Soay sheep in 1958 and has been closely associated with the work ever since, staying on Hirta frequently and visiting Soay, Boreray and Dùn occasionally. He has kept a small flock of Soay sheep in England and was a founder of the Rare Breeds Survival Trust.

JOHN C SMYTH is Emeritus Professor of Biology in the University of Paisley and an honorary professor in the Department of Environmental Science, University of Stirling. He is President of the Scottish Environmental Education Council and was Chairman of the Secretary of State for Scotland's Working Group on Environmental Education. Internationally he has been involved for many years with the Commission on Education and Communication of the World Conservation Union (IUCN), has been a consultant for the UNESCO/UNEP programme and was rapporteur to the Working Group on Education, Public Awareness and Training which assembled the material for UNCED's Agenda 21, Chapter 36.

Director's Preface and Acknowledgements

S t Kilda has long been a source of fascination for many people. The story of its inhabitants, and their final abandonment of their homes in 1930, is a poignant reminder of the fragility of small communities living on the edge of the world. Today, St Kilda is bereft of its indigenous population, but has become a centre for study of the natural world. Glasgow Museums staff have a particular interest in the islands, and Meg Buchanan has co-ordinated this interest to produce a book of essays and accompanying exhibition on the continuing story of St Kilda.

I would like to thank The National Trust for Scotland; Scottish Natural Heritage; HM Armed Forces, St Kilda Detachment; the Royal Commission on the Ancient and Historical Monuments of Scotland; Mary Harman and the departments of archaeology of both Durham and Glasgow universities for their support and encouragement in the production of this volume and of the exhibition.

Thanks are due to the following for their assistance in the preparation of this book: Dr J Morton Boyd, CBE, formerly Director (Scotland), Nature Conservancy Council; Mr Douglas Dow, CB, Director, Robin Turner, Archaeologist and Philip Schreiber, Buildings Surveyor, The National Trust for Scotland; Professor J B L Mathews, Director, Mr D J Ellett and colleagues, Scottish Association for Marine Science, Dunstaffnage Marine Laboratory, Oban; Dr Margaret Mackay and the staff of the School of Scottish Studies, University of Edinburgh; Professor Christopher Morris, Department of Archaeology, University of Glasgow; Sam Scott and colleagues, Royal Commission on the Ancient and Historical Monuments of Scotland, and Sue Scott, marine biologist. MacLeod of MacLeod kindly gave permission to use material from the MacLeod Muniments.

Particular thanks must go to the authors, to the staff of Glasgow Museums and to Susan Storrier who acted as temporary research assistant on the project for 3 months.

It has been a pleasure to co-operate once again with Her Majesty's Stationery Office and we extend our thanks to their staff.

JULIAN SPALDING
Director, Glasgow Museums

Introduction

Meg Buchanan

The St Kilda archipelago lies in the Atlantic Ocean, 64 kilometres west of the Sound of Harris. On a clear day the islands are visible from there, offering an irresistible temptation to the adventurous explorer. The archipelago consists of the islands of Hirta, Boreray, Soay and Dùn, and numerous sea stacs and skerries of which Stac an Armin (191 metres high) and Stac Lee (165 metres), the highest in the British Isles, are the most spectacular. These remote islands are home to a rich wildlife and, until 1930, Hirta supported a small population making a living from the produce of the land and the sea.

The landscape of St Kilda has been fashioned by the action of volcanoes, ice, wind and water. About 60 million years ago, a rift in the northern continent consisting of present-day Europe, America and Greenland caused widespread volcanic activity, including that centred on St Kilda (at the same time initiating the opening of the Atlantic Ocean). The centre of the volcano, sited between Hirta and Boreray, has collapsed inwards. The gabbro rocks forming St Kilda's jagged, eroded cliffs and sea stacs were produced during the earliest phases of activity, while the rounded inland contours of the main island, Hirta, result from weathering of later intrusive granophyre masses.

Weather patterns on St Kilda are strongly influenced by the North Atlantic Drift. Winters are mild and summers cool. The islands are exposed to Atlantic depressions and experience high rainfall and strong winds. The prevailing wind is south-westerly and often blows at force 3 or less. However, gales with gusts of over 100 knots are not uncommon, and severely restrict movement on the islands.

Soils are acid and peaty. The vegetation is mainly grassland, enriched in places by seabird droppings, with wind-blasted heather communities. Trees are absent, except for the tiny Least willow which grows to about 5 cm in height. There is bilberry, crowberry and cowberry, but there are no gorse bushes. Vivid patches of

Figure 1.   Village Bay showing the rounded granite contours of Oiseval and the rugged Dùn gabbro.

colour are created by flowering plants, especially thrift, primrose, roseroot, purple saxifrage and yellow flag. In the derelict arable ground of Village Bay is luxurious grassland containing buttercups and daisies. On Dùn, the only island on the archipelago not grazed by feral sheep, but enriched by seabird manure, vegetation is rank. Sorrel and wild angelica abound.

St Kilda is one of the major seabird breeding areas in the North Atlantic. On Boreray and the stacs is the world's largest colony of gannets. About half the British population of puffins nests in burrows on Dùn, Soay, Boreray and the steep, grassy slopes of Hirta. There too, Manx shearwaters, storm petrels and Leach's petrels are present. St Kilda has the largest colony of fulmars in the British Isles. They nest mainly on the Hirta cliffs, although they are beginning to colonise Village Bay. The other seabirds are rarely seen in Village Bay. There, oystercatchers and eider ducks are common.

A familiar sound at night in the Village is the drumming of snipe. During the day, the St Kilda wren can be heard singing as it perches on the ruined Village chimney tops. The wren is a sub-species, larger than its mainland relative. Other breeding land birds are starlings and rock pipits. Migrants include wagtails,

Figure 2.   Buttercups and Yellow Flag in the Village Meadows.

meadow pipits and geese. One bird no longer seen in the islands, or anywhere else, is the extinct Great Auk. The last one recorded on St Kilda was killed on Stac an Armin in 1840: the last in the world was killed in Iceland in 1844.

Today, there are few animal species on St Kilda. The house mouse did not survive the evacuation of the population, and had died out by 1931. The field mouse, on the other hand, has prospered. It is much larger than the Scottish mainland field mouse and weighs over 70 grammes when fully grown. It may have been brought to St Kilda by Norsemen. As a protected species, it roams St Kilda unmolested and, although not previously a carnivore, it now feeds on the carcasses of birds and sheep. Its principal food includes snails, insects, moss and seeds. Common seals are frequently seen around the islands, and a few breed on suitable sites.

The Soay sheep on St Kilda are an internationally important feral group. Until the evacuation they were kept on Soay only, but in 1932 a flock of 107 was moved to Hirta. The less well-known flock of Hebridean Blackface sheep on Boreray is probably one of the few remaining examples of pure bred Blackface in the British Isles. Other flocks have been interbred with Cheviots and other breeds.

Figure 3.   St Kilda wren photographed by Cherry Kearton in 1896.

Figure 4.   Cartoon by John Clarke, first drawn for the St Kilda Mail, 1992.

Until the evacuation in 1930, the St Kildans exploited the produce of the islands as tenants of a distant landlord. Today, the remains of their dwellings and storage cleitean are a poignant reminder of that community. Before the 1830s the islanders lived in a cluster of houses somewhere to the north and east of the present Village. It is likely that the village was rebuilt many times, and its location may have changed. It is first illustrated in a watercolour of 1812 by Sir Thomas Dyke Acland, landowner and MP for Devon, who visited the islands in that year accompanied by his wife. The small stone-built houses with thatched roofs were typical of Hebridean housing at that time. Humans and cattle shared a windowless one-room house with a central hearth, the cattle separated from the humans by a low wall or talan. Bed spaces were built into the thick walls. There was little furniture and there were few household goods. Land was divided according to the run-rig system, each tenant's plots being scattered throughout the whole arable area. These plots were re-allocated at regular intervals.

The changes brought about by the Reverend Neil MacKenzie in the 1830s, part of the general reform of agriculture in Scotland at this time, secured each tenant

Figure 5.   *Village and bay from the south by Sir Thomas Dyke Acland, 1812. The village is depicted as a small cluster of buildings to the north of the present Street.*

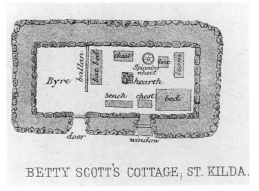

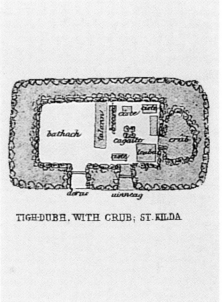

Figure 6. *Plans of two black houses built in the 1830s. Both have accommodation for cattle, and one has an old-style crûb or wall bed.*

Figure 7. *A scatter of cleitean in the Village area.*

Figure 8.   St Kildans landing stores. Photographed by Cherry Kearton in 1896.

his own strip of land on which his house was built. Gifts from well-wishers of windows, furniture, and crockery helped furnish the houses to a standard superior to that enjoyed by most Hebridean islanders.

The St Kilda dwelling-houses did not have farm buildings attached to them in the same way as lowland farmsteads, but small stone-built cleitean acted as storage for dried birds, hay, fuel and other supplies. Seasonal dwellings and bothies were used for temporary work away from the Village.

The St Kildans exploited the resources of the whole archipelago, using small boats to move between the islands and stacs, and landing people to work on them. These boats were vital to the economy of the islands. They were communally-owned for most of the islands' history, but latterly groups of families shared a boat. Until a jetty was built in 1901, the boats had to be hauled out of the water when not in use. When, in the 1930s, the islanders could no longer find sufficient able-bodied people to man a boat, their fate was inevitable.

On land, there were no roads or wheeled vehicles, nor is there evidence of slypes or sledges being used to haul produce. Until the mid 19th century horses were kept for carrying fuel – peat or turf – as there was no wood on the island.

Otherwise the islanders carried everything on their backs. This may help explain the scatter of storage cleitean throughout the islands as intermediate stops on the long journey home.

To feed themselves and pay the rent, the islanders grew crops of barley and oats, tilling the ground with hand tools, not ploughs. For home consumption they grew cabbages, and from the late 18th century a wider range of vegetables including potatoes, carrots and turnips. Rhubarb was grown, and in 1896 the minister, Mr Fiddes, grew strawberries.

Cattle were kept on Hirta and hay was cut for winter fodder. Blackface sheep were kept on Hirta and Boreray. Ewes' milk was used in making cheese, and the wool for cloth: clothing, blanketing and tweed. Cheese, mutton and tweed were exported, the last also being sold to tourists. (The Soay sheep on the island of Soay were the property of the proprietor.)

The islanders fished from the rocks and from their boats, but were not overfond of eating fish and exported little until the late 19th century. They were, above all, fowlers. Gannets, puffins, fulmars, guillemots and razorbills provided flesh, and in some cases eggs, for home consumption and for sale. (Gannet or 'best solan goose' sold in Edinburgh in 1642 for twenty shillings Scots. Best grouse was 13/4d, best hen 8/- and a pair of best rabbits 16/-.)[1] Puffin and fulmar feathers were used to pay the rent, being exported as stuffing for mattresses and pillows. Until 1878 the fulmar bred nowhere in Britain except on St Kilda, giving the islanders a monopoly of its produce. The fulmar provided not only food and feathers but oil which it spits at intruders. This was a valuable commodity collected by the St Kildans and sold for use as a machine oil.

Markets for St Kildan produce changed over time. By the late 19th century there was little demand for dried seabirds or fulmar oil. The islanders made more tweed and knitted socks to sell to the tourists. (Knitting was introduced by Mrs Buchan, the minister's wife, in the early 18th century.) Their own diet was changing too as they took fewer birds from the cliffs, importing instead tea, jam and wheat flour.

The St Kildans were of Hebridean stock. They spoke Gaelic, but soon learned some English when visiting yachtsmen and tourists made it prudent to do so. (There was a school on the island from 1884.) They dressed in a similar fashion to other islanders. There are records of early Christian churches on Hirta, and in the 17th century the minister from Harris travelled to Hirta each year with the factor. While the factor collected the rents, he performed weddings and baptisms. From the 18th century ministers and missionaries were provided and a new church and manse were built in the early 19th century. In 1843, at the Disruption, the islanders joined the Free Church of Scotland and in 1900 the United Free Church.

Early observers record that the islanders loved music and games, engaging in horse racing and playing a form of shinty. Poems recorded by the Reverend Neil MacKenzie praised the skills of the men on the cliffs. In the mid 19th century the St Kildans were drawn to evangelical religion and their move to the Free Church brought with it an austerity in their cultural life. During the ministry of John MacKay, 1865-89, music and games were discouraged and long hours were spent in church.

The St Kildan population reduced through emigration and infant tetanus in the 19th and 20th centuries, and eventually it became clear that the remaining islanders would have to leave. They were evacuated at their own request in August 1930. Most were settled in Morvern, working for the Forestry Commission. The abandoned islands were purchased in 1931 by Lord Dumfries, later fifth Marquess of Bute, as a bird reserve. He encouraged the St Kildans to return home for summer trips, and permitted visits by some tourists and naturalists. However, the islands lay unprotected, at the mercy of sheltering trawlermen, and other unsympathetic visitors who might plunder them for souvenirs.

Figure 9a.   Finlay McQueen seated outside his house. Early 20th century.

Figure 9b.   'St Kilda Maids and Matrons' photographed by Norman McLeod of the George Washington Wilson Studio, 1886.

Figure 10.   Operation Hardrock 1957. The military encampment in the Village Meadows. The Church and Manse are in the left foreground: the Village Street is just visible behind the encampment.

The Marquess, a keen ornithologist, was anxious to secure the future of the islands, and offered them in his will to The National Trust for Scotland. On 30 March 1957 the Trust took the courageous decision to accept responsibility for the future well-being of St Kilda, declared the islands inalienable, and leased them to the Nature Conservancy Council as a National Nature Reserve. This decision came just in time to save the Village. Before his death, the Marquess of Bute had agreed to sub-lease small areas of Hirta to the War Office as a radar tracking station for its new missile launching base in South Uist. The army proposed to build accommodation in the south-east corner of Village Bay, and to construct a road from there to the summit of Mullach Mór where the station would be built. The road was to cut through the Village, the islanders' houses were to be demolished and the building stones used as bottoming for the road. Fortunately, representatives from The National Trust for Scotland and the Nature Conservancy Council had accompanied the military personnel to St Kilda on this Operation Hardrock and were able to negotiate an alternative route for the road. The Village was saved.

The presence of the army on the islands is a mixed blessing. The army camp is an intrusion in the St Kildan landscape. The use of landing craft which, in summer, transport stores and personnel to the islands, unloading on the storm beach, risks the accidental introduction of rats to St Kilda. This would have a devastating effect, especially on ground-nesting birds. On the other hand, the year-round presence of the army on Hirta has been crucial to the protection of the islands. The army provides an infrastructure of power, water supply, logistics transport and medical aid which facilitates the work of the conservation bodies.

The National Trust for Scotland assumes direct responsibility for the maintenance of the built environment of St Kilda. Many of the buildings and archaeological remains are protected under the Ancient Monuments Acts of 1963 and 1972. The Trusts' St Kilda Management Plan, 1990,[2] has informally extended this protection to the whole island group. The Trust is required to provide public access to its properties. This is rather difficult on St Kilda. Visiting yachtsmen and cruise ships are welcome. To allow others to enjoy the islands, and to maintain the Village and other buildings, the Trust sends volunteer work parties to St Kilda in the summer months. Groups of twelve people spend a fortnight on Hirta. Until

Figure 11.   *National Trust for Scotland work party members rebuilding the roof of House 6.*

the 1980s these volunteers undertook a programme of maintenance, largely in the Village, and restored five of the 1860s houses to provide accommodation and workshop space for themselves.

In 1983, the Trust entered into discussions with the Historic Buildings and Monuments Directorate of the Scottish Development Department (now Historic Scotland) about future conservation of the buildings and investigation of archaeological remains. It was agreed that to allow further repairs to the structures, and gain a better understanding and interpretation of St Kilda in advance of excavation, a detailed survey of the built environment was required. The Royal Commission on the Ancient and Historical Monuments of Scotland was invited to undertake this work to provide a survey on which applications to investigate and restore the protected sites could be based. In parallel with this, the Trust invited Durham University's Department of Archaeology to carry out a programme of archaeological investigation on the islands. Both bodies sent professional staff to St Kilda to work with and supervise the Trust's annual work parties.

Care for the natural environment of St Kilda is the responsibility of Scottish Natural Heritage (formerly the Nature Conservancy Council for Scotland and the Countryside Commission for Scotland). A warden spends the spring and summer months on Hirta, ensuring that the islands are respected by their summer visitors, and gathering information on the wildlife. He is based in the Factor's House, now the Scottish Natural Heritage headquarters on St Kilda. This, with the Store, provides accommodation and a working base for the many natural scientists who visit St Kilda to carry out routine bird counts and undertake research projects.

St Kilda is a National Nature Reserve. It has also been designated a Biosphere Reserve (1976), a National Scenic Area (1981), a Site of Special Scientific Interest (1984) and a European Community Special Protection Area (1992). In recognition of its quality as both a nature reserve and a historic site, St Kilda was declared Scotland's first World Heritage Site in 1986.

Much has been written on the history of St Kilda before the evacuation of the population in 1930. The work of conservationists and scientists on the islands in the years since 1930 is less well known, except through scientific publications. The aim of this volume is to redress that balance. It is written for the general reader with an all-round interest in St Kilda and its human and other inhabitants. The aim is not simply to report the results of scientific investigation, but to give a flavour of how this work is done and of the trials and tribulations of applying scientific methods on St Kilda. It is by no means a comprehensive survey of research projects on St Kilda, but a personal view of this work by some of the major researchers.

Mary Harman sets the scene. She has an outstanding knowledge of the islands. For her doctoral thesis,[3] she explored the history of the St Kildans. In this essay she looks at St Kilda through the eyes of the many visitors who have observed and written about it. Their works provide an unparalleled record of the settlement of this group of Scottish islands.

Geoffrey Stell describes the work of the Royal Commission on the detailed recording of the buildings. The resultant publication[4] provides a baseline for future investigations, and a snapshot of the condition of the buildings against which future change can be monitored.

Norman Emery and Alex Morrison discuss the work of the archaeologists on St Kilda. This work is the beginning of a long process of exploration of the islands' history, especially the early period for which there are no historical records. Modern archaeological investigation results in much more than the uncovering of building remains and artefacts. The authors show that excavation produces useful biological information relating to the St Kildans' use and development of plants and animals. They show, too, that archaeology need not be destructive, and that much can be learned about the structures on the islands by geophysical and other forms of ground survey.

Mark Tasker describes the major studies on the seabirds and marine life of St Kilda. For their future wellbeing, it is crucial to understand the effects of pollution and increased industrial fishing on the marine community. This community may soon be threatened by deep sea oil drilling in the seas between the Hebrides and Rockall, and by re-routing of oil tankers near to St Kilda.

Peter Jewell discusses the Soay sheep population on Hirta. Long-term investigation has produced a wealth of information on this group, information which has important implications for the study and preservation of feral groups of animals throughout the world. The study has benefited from new discoveries in science such as DNA mapping which will allow a clearer understanding of the breeding success and fitness of individual Soays within the population.

John Smyth concludes with a reflection on our responsibilities towards St Kilda, and hence to the world in general. His essay is a stark reminder that the future well-being of St Kilda is inextricably bound to the future good health of the world at large. We all have a part to play in ensuring that.

The naturalist James Fisher wrote in 1947 'Whatever he studies, the future observer of St Kilda will be haunted the rest of his life by the place, and tantalised by the impossibility of describing it, to those who have not seen it'.[5] Perhaps these essays will go some way towards describing St Kilda as it was, and as it is today as a unique outdoor laboratory for historical and scientific research.

Notes and References

[1] Sprott, Gavin 1993 'From Fowling to Poaching' ed Cheape, H *Tools and Traditions: Studies in European Ethnology presented to Alexander Fenton* NMS, Edinburgh.

[2] National Trust for Scotland 1990 *St Kilda Management Plan 1990–94*, Edinburgh.

[3] Harman, Mary 1994 *The History and Culture of the St Kildans to 1930* Unpublished PhD thesis, University of Edinburgh.

[4] Stell, Geoffrey P and Harman, Mary 1988 *Buildings of St Kilda* RCAHMS, Edinburgh.

[5] Fisher, James 1968 'St Kilda: A Natural Experiment' *New Naturalists Journal* vol 1.

Chapter 1

The History of St Kilda

Mary Harman

There are many days when St Kilda is visible from the Outer Hebrides, and though we do not know when man first reached St Kilda, it seems likely that four or five thousand years ago, during the Neolithic period, people from Harris or Uist would have explored the islands. There may have been seasonal visits to harvest seabirds, or to establish long term settlement, though as yet no evidence has been found to support this.

During the reconstruction of the village in the late 1830s, numerous gnocan sithichean or 'fairy hillocks' were removed. These were found to be cairns covering 'stone coffins . . . formed of four flat stones set on edge and covered by a fifth' or 'formed of several stones set in the same way'. The 'coffins' contained pieces of pottery; bones were recognised in some of them. This brief description indicates the discovery of a group of cist burials which may well have been of Bronze Age date,[1] implying settlement in the second millennium BC.

Groups of stones set into the ground and apparently forming boat shapes have been recognised in An Lag bho'n Tuath, together with several small cairns. Material from a small excavation in one of the stone settings yielded a C14 date of 3807 years ago (uncorrected), and it has been suggested that they may be the remains of graves dating to the Bronze Age,[2] but the dated material may not be contemporary with the setting. Further work currently being undertaken may clarify the date and purpose of these structures.

In about 1840 an 'earth house' or souterrain, known as Taigh an t-Sithiche or 'the Fairy's House' was found and covered again. It was first investigated in 1875, and again in 1897, 1927 and 1974: it can still be seen today. Objects found in it include an iron spearhead, sherds of pottery (some of them dateable to the Iron Age) and crude stone tools. This type of structure occurs in Scotland in association with Iron Age houses, and together with the pottery it confirms that people were living on St Kilda in the first half of the first millennium AD. Settlers on the islands would have brought domestic animals with them, so ancestors of the Soay sheep were grazing St Kilda about two thousand years ago or earlier. As we do not know how often new stock was introduced to the islands by later immigrants, it would be unwise to regard the Soay sheep as a breed which has not changed since prehistoric times.

Early Religious Communities

From the late 6th to the 9th centuries AD early Christian scholars and missionaries travelled between Ireland and the west coast of Scotland and beyond, even as far as Iceland. Small islands were favourite places for establishing religious communities, and though the evidence is slim, the chapels of St Columba, St Brendan and Christ Church, first recorded in the 17th century,[3] may have been founded at this time. They were all built in the same way and were thatched like the houses; each one had a churchyard. There is no trace of these to be seen now. Christ Church stood within the walls of an oval burial ground; the same shape of enclosure is found at other early Christian sites in Scotland and

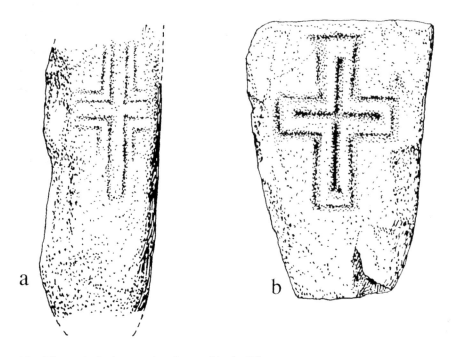

Figure 12.   The two incised crosses found re-used in the Village.

Ireland. Two stones with crosses cut into them have been found built into later structures, one in the front wall of House 16 and one in the roof of a cleit above Black House R. They are similar to crosses found elsewhere, some of early Christian date and some of Norse date. Altogether, it seems likely that when the Norsemen first went to St Kilda, they found a Christian community, possibly guided by a group of monks.

Scandinavian Influences

Scandinavian raiders were first recorded on the west coast of Scotland at the end of the 8th century, and were soon followed by settlers. Norse settlement and influence was so great in the Hebrides that by the end of the 11th century the islands had become part of the Norse Kingdom of Man and the Isles. A number of place names on St Kilda are directly of Norse origin, rather than Gaelic words derived from Norse: examples are Ruaival (Red Hill); the Cambir (crest or ridge); Soay (Sheep Island). In the 19th century, a spearhead, sword and whetstone were found in a mound, almost certainly a burial deposit, the bones having decayed in the acid soil. A pair of Norse brooches of 9th or 10th century date may well have come from another grave.[4] Finds from the recent archaeological excavations include pieces of soapstone (page 41), probably imported during the Norse period.[5]

According to one of the sagas, an Icelandic bishop, driven south by storms on a voyage to Norway in 1202, visited 'the islands that are called Hirtir'. If the identification of Hirtir with St Kilda is correct, this would be the earliest literary reference to the islands.[6]

Norse supremacy in the isles ceased after the Battle of Largs in 1263, but the Lords of the Isles continued to rule the Hebrides and parts of the west coast until the Lordship of the Isles was forfeit to the Crown in 1493. In 1346 John of Islay granted to his son, Reginald, various lands and islands, including St Kilda.[7] John of Fordun, writing later in the 14th century, described 'Hirth' as 'the best stronghold in all the islands' and noted that wild sheep which could only be caught by hunters were said to exist on an island nearby.[8]

Changes in Ownership

Although the charter of 1346 indicates that St Kilda was in the hands of the MacDonalds, by 1549, when Donald Monro was writing about the diocese of Argyll and the Isles, it had passed into the hands of the MacLeods of Harris and Dunvegan.[9] The MacLeods continued to own it until the late 18th century. In 1772 Norman MacLeod of MacLeod inherited from his grandfather an estate burdened by debt. The sale of Harris, including St Kilda, in 1779 to a distant cousin, Alexander MacLeod of Berneray, went some way towards resolving the financial problems.[10] Alexander MacLeod's son sold St Kilda in 1804 to Colonel Donald MacLeod of Achnagoyle and Colbost, son of one of the earlier missionaries.[11] He and his son, John MacPherson MacLeod of Glendale, were sympathetic proprietors. In 1871 St Kilda was bought by Norman MacLeod of MacLeod, and continued in the hands of the MacLeods of Dunvegan until 1931, when it was sold to Lord Dumfries.[12] *Bute*

Since the earliest records, the rent due to the proprietors was paid in kind; mainly feathers, fulmar oil, dried birds, dried meat, barley, butter, cheese and wool. When MacLeod of Achnagoyle and Colbost bought the island, the range of commodities was reduced to feathers, but later a wider range of goods was used to pay the rent. Records of the rent paid by individual households survive from the early 1870s, and provide information about the goods supplied by each family and the island as a whole. Figure 13a shows the goods used in the payment of rent from 1873. It shows that the production of quantities of cheese ceased in the 1890s, and that after the war the diminishing numbers of households paid their rent only in cash, cattle and tweed, and rarely in feathers and fish.[13]

Early Accounts of the Islands

There are three brief accounts written in the 16th century: those of Hector Boece, published in 1527, Donald Monro, written about 1549, and an anonymous report written between 1577 and 1595.[14] Between them, they reported that St Kilda could only be visited when the sea was calm, but every year a priest or minister visited the islands to perform marriages and baptise children born in the previous year, and either he or MacLeod's factor collected the rent. The people cultivated the land and kept sheep and cattle, but depended on collecting seabirds and their eggs for much of their food. All three authors comment on the number of sheep to be found there.

Similar accounts by Sir Robert Moray,[15] a founder member of the Royal Society, and another by Sir George MacKenzie of Tarbat,[16] a relative of the MacLeods, may have aroused the curiosity of Martin Martin, a Skyeman who was tutor to the MacLeods and remained a friend of the family. He accompanied the minister of Harris, John Campbell, on his annual visit in 1697, and afterwards wrote *A Late Voyage to St Kilda, the remotest of all the Hebrides or Western Isles of Scotland*, which was published in 1698. Further editions and reprints have appeared to the present day (Figure 14). This was a detailed account of the islands and the way of life of the people, together with information about the seabirds on which they depended. These included the fulmar, which at that time nested only in St Kilda, and was thus a very rare bird in the British Isles. Martin also described

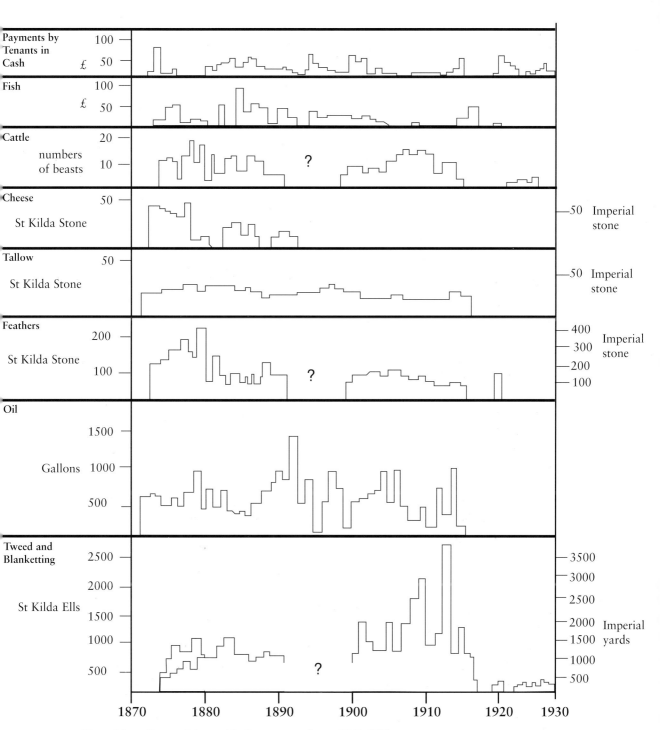

Figure 13a. Commodities used in the payment of rent, 1870–1930.

5

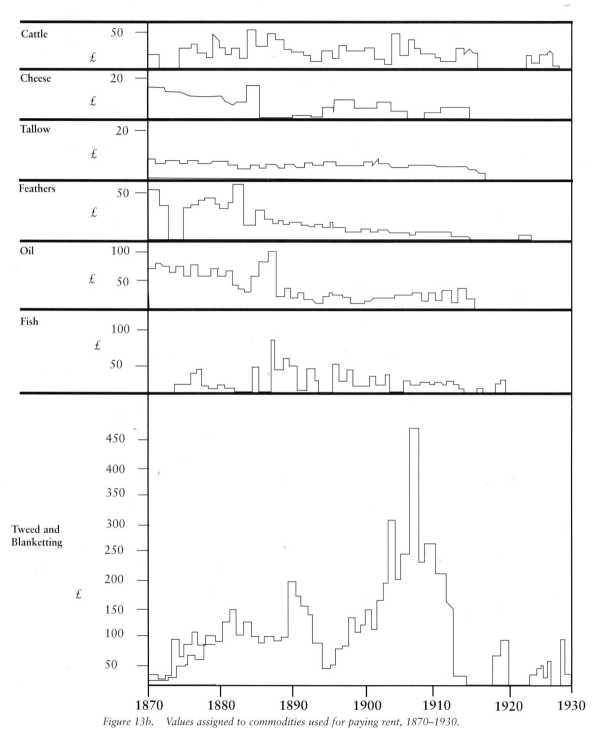

Figure 13b.   Values assigned to commodities used for paying rent, 1870–1930.

the career of one of the islanders who foisted himself upon the community as a religious leader, claiming to be directed by John the Baptist. Campbell and Martin took him back to Skye to prevent his continuing his perverted religion on the island. Martin's book was the first literary identification of the islands as St Kilda: and ever since, the name St Kilda has superseded Hirta, except among Gaelic speakers. In 1703 Martin published another book about the Hebrides, including a shorter account of St Kilda.[17]

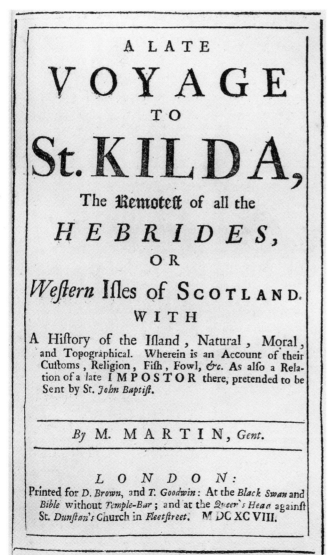

These two books probably aroused public interest in St Kilda, and in 1704, after the General Assembly of the Church of Scotland had decided to send someone to the island to give the people religious instruction, Alexander Buchan travelled from Thurso to Edinburgh to offer his services. He spent the next twenty-five years attending to both the spiritual welfare and the education of his little flock; when the Church funds failed, he was supported by the newly founded Society in Scotland for the Propagation of Christian Knowledge, and in 1710 he was ordained minister in Edinburgh. When Martin's book went out of print, Buchan published in 1727 a small book consisting largely of extracts from Martin's

Figure 14. Title page: Martin Martin's 'A Late Voyage to St Kilda'.

book, along with an account of his own ministry and some observations about the St Kildans. Revised editions of this book continued to appear after Buchan's death in 1729.

Population

In 1697 there were 180 people, the maximum recorded population (Figure 15).[18] Buchan's account indicates that after payment of rent in kind, the resources available could not support this number, and many died of malnutrition. The weakened population was struck down by smallpox in 1727, and only 30 people survived, most of them children. Eleven of the survivors were men and boys who had been put on Stac an Armin to catch birds. As there were not enough people left on Hirta able to man a boat to collect them, they were marooned there for the winter. The islanders' plight was only discovered when the factor's boat arrived in 1728.[19] People from Skye, Harris and North Uist were settled in the island,[20] and by 1758 the population had risen to 88.[21] By 1800 there were about 100 people on St Kilda;[22] in the following 50 years the recorded numbers fluctuated between 92[23] and 110,[24] but in 1852, 36 people emigrated to Australia[25] and thereafter the number did not rise above 77.[26] From the 1890s there were some individuals,

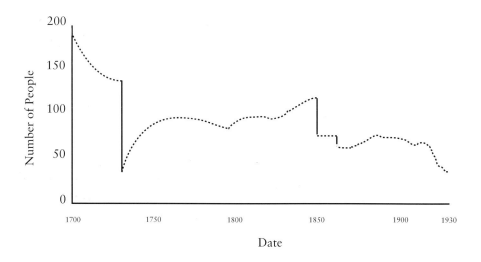

Figure 15. *Population figures 1697–1930.*

mainly young people, who left to settle on other islands or the mainland; after the war, emigration increased, with one large family moving to Lewis; 17 people left in the 1920s. By 1925 the population had fallen to 46 people, and in 1930 there were only 36 to be evacuated.

The earliest indications of a high infant mortality occur in Buchan's account, and though that may have been the result of malnutrition, it is clear that by 1758 it was common for babies to die at about eight days old, from infant tetanus.[27] This terrible disease was largely responsible for the lack of increase in numbers in the 19th century; 160 births were recorded between 1831 and 1891, and of these, 92 babies died within the first few weeks of life. Some couples raised only a few of many children born to them, and women ceased to make any special provision for clothing their babies until they had survived the first critical weeks.[28] In the 1890s the provision of a nurse and the careful supervision of the new-born by the minister helped to ensure their survival, and the last recorded case of tetanus was in 1892.[29]

Eighteenth Century Visitors

After Alexander Buchan's death in 1729, for the next century spiritual care of the community fell to a succession of catechists and missionaries, some of whom were poorly qualified. The chapels fell into disuse and the people worshipped in a barn or store.

Kenneth MacAulay, minister of Harris, visited the island in 1758 to report on the work of the missionary, and afterwards wrote *The History of St Kilda* published in 1764, with information on the history and cultural life of the people and the natural history of the islands. MacAulay, like Martin before him, regarded the island as a miniature Utopia. Strangely, he did not refer in his book to two events connected with the Jacobite cause. In 1730 Rachel Erskine and her husband, Lord Erskine of Grange, were separated, though both continued to live in Edinburgh. Probably as a result of her provocative behaviour and threats to accuse him of complicity in a Jacobite plot, she was kidnapped in 1732 and sent first to Heisker, North Uist, and two years later to St Kilda. There she endured a miserable existence for eight years before she was removed to Skye where she died in 1745. The secret of her abduction and different hiding-places became public knowledge by the end of the century.[30] During the search for Charles Edward Stuart after his defeat at Culloden in 1746, there was some suspicion that he might have been hiding on the island, and government troops were landed on St Kilda to look for him.[31]

In the 17th and 18th centuries the islands were occasionally visited by fishermen, some of them foreign, but they left no records, and accounts by

MacCulloch and MacKenzie suggest that visitors were rare until well into the 19th century. Captain Alexander MacLeod of Berneray spent considerable sums on improvements in Harris to encourage the fishing industry, and as he sent boats to fish around St Kilda, there may have been more contact with Harris in the late 18th century. He may have built the Store on St Kilda in connection with his fishery scheme.[32]

Nineteenth Century Visitors

There are records of expeditions by members of the aristocracy in 1797, 1799 and 1800.[33] In 1815 MacCulloch found that more than a year had passed since anyone had visited the island.[34] In the 1820s Dr John MacDonald of Ferintosh, 'the Apostle of the North', made three visits to the island, instructing the people in Christianity and encouraging them to practise their faith. He raised funds for the building of a new Church and Manse, which were designed by Robert Stevenson of the Northern Lighthouse service and completed by 1830, when MacDonald accompanied a new minister, Neil MacKenzie, to the island.[35] In 1831 George Clayton Atkinson, a natural historian, visited.[36] Though many of

Figure 16. 'Principal Square in the Capital of St Kilda' by Sir Thomas Dyke Acland, 1812.

these people wrote accounts of their visits and their impressions of the islands, only those by MacCulloch and Atkinson were published at the time.

Several authors agree that the factor in the late 18th and early 19th centuries was exacting an unreasonable proportion of the island's produce in rent, leaving the people with inadequate provision for their own needs. MacLeod of Achnagoyle took the rent only in feathers, and the circumstances of the people were considerably improved.[37]

Neil MacKenzie, minister from 1830 to 1843, was an energetic man who was responsible for great changes in the lives of the St Kildans. Distressed by the squalid condition of the people's homes, he encouraged them to build new and improved houses. The old run-rig system of lotting the arable land was abandoned and each family built a new house on a permanently allotted strip; the cluster of houses making up the old village (Figure 16) was demolished and the new linear Village built along a street running across the strips. Sir Thomas Dyke Acland, who visited the island in 1812 and in 1834, gave £20 to which was added funds raised on the mainland to purchase a window and new furniture for each household.

Religion

Having attended to the physical welfare of the islanders, MacKenzie tackled their spiritual well-being. In 1838 some people were admitted to the church as communicants for the first time, but not until 1841 did he feel that he had wrought true spiritual reform amongst his flock. MacKenzie's notes on life in St Kilda were written up and published by his son in 1911.[38] His collection of twenty songs, many of them laments for people who had died while fowling, was published in 1906.[39]

At the Disruption in 1843 the islanders voted to join the Free Church of Scotland. No one was sent to carry on MacKenzie's work until 1856, when a catechist, Duncan Kennedy, went out for a few years. In 1865 another minister, John MacKay, went to St Kilda. He lacked MacKenzie's youthful vigour, and his housekeeper exerted considerable influence over him and thus over the population as a whole. Apart from increasing the number of services and insisting on a rigorous observation of the Sabbath and attendance at his long services, MacKay's attitude seems chiefly to have been one of passive neglect.[40] In 1889 he was replaced by a younger man, Angus Fiddes, who went to considerable trouble to try to prevent the deaths of babies from tetanus.[41]

When Fiddes left in 1902, he was followed by several missionaries, mostly young men, some with families, who generally stayed for two or three years, though the Camerons stayed for seven years in the 1920s.[42]

Education

When Martin explained the system of writing to the St Kildans in 1697, they could not envisage ever being able to read and write themselves,[43] but Alexander Buchan taught several during his ministry.[44] When MacAulay visited, only a few were literate,[45] but in 1822 a teacher was sent out by the Society for the Support of Gaelic Schools, and by his own account he had considerable success, with a number of pupils being able to read the Bible before he left in 1829.[46] MacKenzie continued with this work.[47] Duncan Kennedy's niece Anne taught for a few years around 1860.[48] The 1872 Education Act passed St Kilda by, but for several years from 1884 the Ladies' Highland Association sent a succession of young men, mostly students, who stayed for a summer or a year and taught in the Church or in a room in the Factor's House, where they were lodged.[49] In 1898 a schoolroom was added to the Church. From the early 20th century the missionaries or their wives took on the job of teaching as well, and the St Kilda School came within the Inverness Education authority, receiving annual visits from His Majesty's Inspectors of Schools.[50]

Further Visitors

In 1834 the first steam yacht visited St Kilda,[51] and in 1838 another, with over 30 visitors aboard, went to the island.[52] Few travellers were wealthy enough to have their own boat, but despite the difficulties in arranging for transport, the number of visitors increased, and included people whose main concern was the natural history of the islands, such as MacGillivray and Milner.[53]

In the 1860s Captain Otter of the *Porcupine*, a vessel surveying for the first Admiralty chart of the area, befriended the people of St Kilda.[54] He carried several visitors, including the Duke of Atholl; Alexander Carmichael, who recorded several Gaelic songs, and Captain Thomas, who described some of the buildings and for whom Anne Kennedy collected several tales from one of the oldest inhabitants, Euphemia MacCrimmon.[55] A severe storm in October 1860 almost resulted in the loss of the *Porcupine,* and swept away the islanders' boat, several roofs and much of the harvest. Otter made a public appeal for funds to help the islanders. The Royal Highland and Agricultural Society of Scotland had in 1859 been entrusted with money bequeathed by a Mr Kelsall to be used to assist the St Kildans, and from this the Society contributed to the purchase of supplies and household goods which Otter carried to St Kilda. In order to avoid the people becoming recipients of charity, it was arranged that they should exchange work for goods, and an agreement was drawn up whereby the men were to build new houses for their families and for the elderly and infirm. Sir John MacPherson MacLeod assumed the responsibility for arranging for masons to go from Skye to

Passengers booked through by Carron Company's Steamers.

GLASGOW AND THE HIGHLANDS.

STEAMER

"DUNARA
CASTLE."
453 Tons.

WEEKLY CIRCULAR TOUR

BY THE FAVOURITE STEAMER

"DUNARA CASTLE,"

From GLASGOW, every Thursday, at 2 p.m., and
from GREENOCK, at 7 p.m., for

COLONSAY, IONA, MULL, TYREE, SKYE, HARRIS, UIST, and BARRA.

Returning to GLASGOW on Wednesday morning.

The scenery is most varied, and is unequalled for solitary grandeur, and wild and savage magnificence. It teems with incidents romantic and tragic which have been rendered famous by the pens of the historian, the poet, and the novelist. Glimpses are to be had of the primitive ways of life that are fast becoming obsolete.

Cabin Fare for the Round, - - - £1 15s.
Do.   do.   (including Meals), £3 5s.

Occasional Special Trips to the Island of St. Kilda.
Return Cabin Fare, including Meals, £4 4s.

Time Bills, with Maps, and Berths secured, on application to
MARTIN ORME, 20 Robertson Street, GLASGOW.

Figure 17. Advertisement for steamer trips, including visits to St Kilda, from the late 1870s.

supervise the work, and between 1861 and 1862 sixteen new houses were built along the Street in a style imported from the mainland.[56]

In 1875 a journalist, John Sands, went to St Kilda. He felt that instead of all goods passing through the hands of the factor, the people should be assisted to sell their produce in the Hebrides and purchase what they needed. Having raised money for a boat suitable for such a voyage, he took this boat to St Kilda in 1876. The factor did not make his usual trip in late summer, so Sands had no return transport and was marooned over the following winter. In January a group of shipwrecked Austrian sailors landed on the island, and were hospitably received by the St Kildans, but their winter supplies were insufficient to sustain the extra numbers, and Sands sent messages asking for help in 'mailboats' - messages sealed in containers and attached to a piece of wood with a sail. After the messages were received in Orkney and Poolewe, an Admiralty boat went with immediate assistance, and took Sands and the Austrians away.[57] Later, in the early summer of 1877, further supplies were sent, bought with money from the Kelsall fund and a contribution from the Austrian government. John MacDiarmid accompanied the supplies and wrote a very useful account of his brief stay, with particular attention to agriculture on the island.[58]

Sands held a public meeting and conducted a correspondence with MacLeod in the press about the condition of the St Kildans.[59] He wrote a book about the island. Public interest was aroused, and it was probably partly as a result of this that the shipping company Martin Orme sailing from Glasgow to the Western Isles announced that their steamer *Dunara Castle* would call at St Kilda in June 1877. In that summer seven vessels called at the island.[60] Martin Orme's steamer made one call the following year, but within a few years there were several regular summer visits by different vessels, making St Kilda much more accessible to the general public. George Seton, one of the passengers on the first call by the *Dunara Castle*, published a comprehensive book about the island in 1878.

Improved education in the late 19th century together with a wider circulation of newspapers and magazines increased knowledge and curiosity about St Kilda. Comparative ease of access on the summer steamers led to an ever increasing number of visitors, though some still went on their own or chartered boats. More articles appeared, not only of a general and repetitive nature in popular publications, but also specialist articles on various aspects of natural history, some of them in journals with a very limited circulation.

Figure 18. Dividing the fulmar catch in 1886. G. W. Wilson Studio.

Some of those who visited the island gave things to the St Kildans, particularly money and sweets, and the people also sold birds' eggs and live and dead specimens of birds to visitors. They demonstrated their skills on the cliffs in return for money. Increasing quantities of tweed were sold on the island rather than being offered as rent. From the 1890s tweed was also sent to Alexander Ferguson, an islander who settled in Glasgow as a tweed merchant, returning each summer to visit his family. Gifts from visitors and from wellwishers on the mainland led increasingly to a reliance on and expectation of charity.

In 1883 the Napier Commission, which undertook an official enquiry into the circumstances of the tenantry in the Highlands and Islands, went to St Kilda to take evidence. In 1885, after a storm, requests for assistance were sent by 'St Kilda mailboats', and though supplies were taken to the island, Malcolm MacNeill reported to the Board of Supervision that there had been no real need.[61] In 1886 a photographer, Norman MacLeod, spent several days on the islands as a result of which the Washington Wilson studio in Aberdeen issued a number of photographs of the islands and the islanders (Figure 18). Among visitors in the

Figure 19. '*St Kildans bartering with the Factor*'. *Photograph by Cherry Kearton, 1896, of islanders paying the rent.*

15

1890s were the Kearton brothers, English naturalists who produced a book in 1897, and two cousins of MacLeod, Norman and Evelyn Heathcote, who published articles and a book in 1900. Both books were generously illustrated with photographs (Figure 19).

Interest on the part of visitors continued in the 20th century. In 1908 and about 1917 brief films were made by Oliver Pike. Longer films with explanatory notes, designed for public showing, were produced in the 1920s.[62]

Communications

The size of the boats used by the St Kildans was dictated by the necessity for lifting a boat out of the sea above the high tide mark to prevent storm damage. In 1860 Captain Otter had constructed a landing place where, with the aid of a crane, the islanders' boat could be lifted out of the sea. This should have allowed the St Kildans to use a boat of a size suitable for crossing to the Hebrides, but a new boat and the landing place were destroyed in the storm of October 1860. In 1878 and again in 1885 the provision of a landing place or slip for drawing up boats was considered, but nothing was done until 1899, when work began on the construction of a jetty, which was finished in 1901.[63] This made the loading and unloading of both goods and passengers much easier.

In the mid 19th century correspondence with relatives in Australia and the Estate was carried twice yearly by the factor for posting in Dunvegan, but once the regular steamer services began there was a more frequent summer postal service, and though the volume of mail was small, in 1900 a Post Office was set up on St Kilda (Figure 20). An irregular winter service was maintained by arrangement with visiting trawlers in the 20th century. Postcards with views of St Kilda and 'the natives' became available in the 20th century and increased the volume of mail, and as more of the islanders settled elsewhere, the demand for a regular winter service arose several times but was never satisfactorily resolved.[64]

The Official View

Until the latter part of the 19th century St Kilda was largely ignored by the Government. The first census in Scotland, in 1841, passed it by, though an enumerator called in 1851 and St Kilda was included in every census from then on. In 1869, when 'An Act for the Preservation of Seabirds' was passed, the St Kildans' dependence on seabirds was recognised, and the Act did not apply to St Kilda. It was replaced in 1880 by a more stringent Act for the 'Protection of Wild Birds', but again, this and subsequent Acts did not apply to St Kilda. In 1904, after concern was raised over the collecting of rare petrels and the St Kilda wrens and their eggs, a special Act was passed to make all previous Acts applicable to St

Kilda, with an exception for the collecting of food species: the St Kildans could continue to take fulmars, gannets, guillemots, puffins and razorbills.

From the 1890s the St Kildans came to the attention of the Scottish Office with increasing frequency. There were probably more Parliamentary Questions asked about the affairs of St Kilda than any other island of comparable size and situation. Perusal of the files reveals a continued reluctance on the part of the Government to become involved in anything which committed them to spending money, except in cases of urgent necessity, when there was a rapid response. When the request came in 1930 for the islanders to be resettled elsewhere, it was clearly a relief.[65]

In 1912 after an alarm over a shortage of supplies, the *Daily Mirror* gave considerable publicity to its own prompt despatch of supplies by chartered boat, and followed this up by establishing a wireless station on the island, for use in emergencies only. In the spring of 1914 they decided to dispose of the wireless, but when war broke out the Admiralty took it over.

From 1915 to 1918 a small naval detachment maintained a watch over the surrounding seas, sending reports of vessels seen back to headquarters in

Figure 20.   St Kilda Post Office. Photographed in 1930 by Alasdair Alpin MacGregor.

17

Stornoway. The steamer service was interrupted but a regular naval supply boat provided the islanders with a frequent mail service, and the young people of the island particularly enjoyed hearing about life on the mainland or in the other islands from the naval servicemen, some of whom were from Lewis. Several young men were employed as watchers. Two St Kildans served in the war, though there was no conscription on the island.[66] In 1918 the island saw enemy action when a U-boat shelled the wireless station. The commander warned the people first to give them time to remove to a safe place. There were no casualties, and the wireless station was soon restored to action.[67]

Decline of the Community

From the late 19th century some St Kildans visited the other Hebridean islands and the mainland. In the 20th century some went to Harris for shopping expeditions. They travelled on the whalers working out of West Loch Tarbert. In 1924 one family left to live in Lewis, and several young people left to find work

Figure 21.   The decaying Village in the late 1930s.

18

on the mainland. Their experiences, together with increased knowledge of the rest of Britain through contact with visitors, led the islanders to wish for a standard of living comparable with that of their neighbours, but this was more than the resources of the island could provide. Demand for assistance from the Government increased, while payment of their rent to the Estate decreased. In 1930, when one large family resolved to emigrate, it was clear that there would not be enough able-bodied people left for the community to continue to live in the way that it had done when it was thriving. The district nurse Wilhelmina Barclay helped the people in reaching their decision to make a final communal request to the Government, for assistance in leaving their island home and for new homes and employment elsewhere.[68]

On 29 August 1930, the 36 remaining islanders were evacuated, along with the district nurse and the missionary and his family, and sent to new homes, mainly in Morvern. As the steamers continued to call at 'the lonely isle' in summer until the outbreak of war in 1939, some islanders were able to revisit their homes and take holidays on the island.

After the Evacuation

There is not known to have been any long-term military presence on St Kilda during the Second World War. Three British planes crashed on the island.[69] After the war, St Kilda was not included in any regular ferry sailings, and it was visited only by fishing boats and travellers fortunate enough to have their own transport.

The Marquess of Bute's bequest of the islands to The National Trust for Scotland in 1956, and the designation as a National Nature Reserve and establishment of the military base in 1957 saw the beginning of a new phase in the history of St Kilda.

Notes and References

1 MacKenzie, Neil 1911 *Episode in the Life of the Rev. Neil MacKenzie, at St Kilda from 1829 to 1843*, ed J B MacKenzie, privately printed, 6–7.
2 Cottam, M B 1979 'Archaeology' ed Small, A *St Kilda Handbook* National Trust for Scotland.
3 Martin, Martin 1753 *A Voyage to St Kilda* 4th edition, Brown and Davis, London, 43–6.
4 Taylor, A B 1967 'The Norsemen on St Kilda' *Saga Book of the Viking Society* 17, 116–44.
5 Emery, Norman 1989 'Excavations on St Kilda' Interim Report in *St Kilda Mail* 13, 16–17.

⁶ Taylor 1967, 120–3.

⁷ Munro, Jean and Munro, R W 1986 *Acts of the Lords of the Isles 1336–1493* Scottish History Society, Edinburgh, 10–11, 209.

⁸ Fordun, John of 1871, 1872 *Chronica Gentis Scotorum* ed W F Skene, Edmonston and Douglas, Edinburgh. vol I, 1871, 44; vol II, 1872, 40.

⁹ Monro, Donald 1961 *Description of the Western Isles of Scotland* ed R W Munro, Oliver and Boyd, Edinburgh, 77–8.

¹⁰ Grant, I F 1959 *The Macleods: The History of a Clan* Faber and Faber, London, 494–508.

¹¹ Seton, George 1878 *St Kilda Past and Present*, Wm. Blackwood and Sons, Edinburgh, 40.

¹² MacLeod Muniments, Dunvegan Castle.

¹³ MacLeod Muniments, Dunvegan Castle.

¹⁴ Anonymous 1595 'The Description of the Isles of Scotland' (probably 1577–95) printed as an appendix to Skene, W F *Celtic Scotland* 1880, vol III, 431–2.

¹⁵ Moray, Robert 1678 'A Description of the Island of Hirta' *Philosophical Transactions of the Royal Society of London* vol 12, 927–9.

¹⁶ MacKenzie, Sir George of Tarbat 1908 'An Account of Hirta and Rona' published in Macfarlane, W *Geographical Collections* Edinburgh, vol III, 28.

¹⁷ Martin, Martin 1716 *A Description of the Western Isles of Scotland*, Bell, Varnam and Osborn, Taylor, Baker and Warner, London (first edition 1703).

¹⁸ Martin 1753, 51.

¹⁹ MacAulay, Kenneth 1764 *The History of St Kilda* Becket and de Hondt, London, 197–8; MacKenzie, Neil 1904 'Antiquities and Old Customs of St Kilda, compiled from notes by the Rev Neil MacKenzie', ed J B MacKenzie, *Proc. Soc. Antiq. Scot.* 38, 1903–4, 399–400.

²⁰ Lawson, W M 1933 *St Kilda and its Church* Bill Lawson Publications, Northton, Isle of Harris, 19–22.

²¹ MacAulay 1764, 196.

²² Clarke, Edward Daniel 1824 *The Life and Remains of Edward Daniel Clarke* ed William Otter, London, 272; Wilson, James 1842 *A Voyage round the Coasts of Scotland and the Isles*, Edinburgh, vol II, 104.

²³ MacLean, Lachlan 1838 *Sketches on the island of St Kilda*, McPhun, Glasgow, 24.

²⁴ MacCulloch, John 1824 *The Highlands and Western Isles of Scotland* London, vol III, 190; Census 1851.

²⁵ Holohan, Ann Maclean 1986 'St Kilda: Emigrants and Disease' *Scottish*

Medical Journal, vol 31, 47–8.

[26] Census 1861; Census 1901.

[27] MacAulay 1764, 199–200.

[28] Lawson pers comm.

[29] Turner, G A 1895 'The Successful Preventive Treatment of the Scourge of St Kilda (*tetanus neonatorum*) with some considerations regarding the management of the cord in the new born infant' *Glasgow Medical Journal* vol 43, March 1895, 161–74.

[30] Laing, D 1876 'An Episode in the Life of Mrs Rachael Erskine, Lady Grange, detailed by herself in a letter from St Kilda, January 20th, 1738' *Proc. Soc. Antiq. Scot.* vol 11, 593–608.

[31] Forbes, Robert 1895, *The Lyon in Mourning,* ed. Henry Paton, Scottish History Society, Edinburgh, vol. I, 162.

[32] Knox, John 1787 *A Tour Through the Highlands of Scotland and the Hebride isles in 1786* London, 158–60.

[33] Clarke 1824; Broughham, Lord 1871 *Memoirs of the Life and Times of Lord Broughham written by himself* London and Edinburgh vol I, 88–112; Wilson 1842, vol I, 3.

[34] MacCulloch, John 1819 *A Description of the Western Isles of Scotland* Hurst, Robinson and Co, London, vol II, 23.

[35] Kennedy, John 1932, *The Apostle of the North; the Life and Labours of the Rev Dr J MacDonald* Northern Counties Newspaper and Printing and Publishing Co, Inverness.

[36] Atkinson, George Clayton 1838 'An Account of an Expedition to St Kilda in 1831' *Trans. Nat. Hist. Soc. Northumberland, Durham and Newcastle* vol 2 215–225 and map p1 III.

[37] MacLeod, Donald 1814 'Notices on the Present State of St Kilda' *Scots Magazine* December 1814, 912–3.

[38] MacKenzie 1911.

[39] MacKenzie, Neil 1906 'Bardachd Irteach' *Celtic Review* vol 2, 328–42.

[40] Ewing, William 1914 *Annals of the Free Church of Scotland,* T&T Clark, vol II, 235; Sands, John 1877 *Out of the world; or, Life in St Kilda* MacLachlan and Stewart, Edinburgh, 29, 115; Connell, Robert 1887 *St Kilda and the St Kildians* Thomas D Morison, London and Glasgow, 21, 37–8, 54–5; MacDiarmid, John 1878 'St Kilda and its inhabitants' *Trans. Highland and Agricultural Soc. Scotland,* vol 10, 234, 241.

[41] Turner 1895 161–74.

[42] MacLachlan, Alice 1906–9 *Diaries.* Typescript copy in National Trust for

Scotland Archive; Cameron, Mary 1973 *Childhood Days on St Kilda* Gairloch; MacLeod, Alexander 1988 'Biographical notes on John MacLeod' Quine, D A *St Kilda Portraits* Frome, 198–213.

[43] Martin 1753, 63.

[44] Buchan, Alexander 1727 *A Description of St Kilda* Edinburgh: Lumisden and Robertson reprinted with substantial alterations by Miss Buchan, 1752, 41–52.

[45] MacAulay 1764, 219.

[46] Gaelic School Reports 1822–6; Kennedy 1932, 284.

[47] MacKenzie 1911, 32.

[48] Royal Highland and Agricultural Society of Scotland Papers: a collection of letters, receipts, etc. relating to the Kelsall Fund.

[49] Scottish Record Office, AF 57/04; Murray, George 1887, *Diary* Typescript extracts in National Trust for Scotland Archive; Ross, John 1890 *St Kilda as it now is.* Manuscript account in National Trust for Scotland Archive.

[50] St Kilda School Log Book.

[51] Carruthers, R 1843 *The Highland notebook; or sketches and anecdotes*, A & C Black, Edinburgh, 255–8.

[52] MacLean 1838, 25.

[53] Atkinson, George Clayton 1831 *A Few Weeks' Ramble among the Hebrides in the Summer of 1831.* Manuscript account, typescript copy in National Trust for Scotland Archive; Atkinson 1838, 215–25; MacGillivray, J 1842 'Account of the Island of St Kilda, chiefly with reference to its natural history' *Edinburgh New Philosophical Journal* vol 32, 47–70; Milner, W M E 1848 'Some Account of the People of St Kilda, and of the Birds in the Outer Hebrides' *The Zoologist*, 2054–62.

[54] Royal Highland and Agricultural Society of Scotland Papers.

[55] Morgan, John E 1861 'The Falcon among the Fulmars; or six hours in St Kilda' *MacMillan's Magazine* June 1861, 104–6; Kennedy, Anne and Thomas, F W L 1874 'Letter from St Kilda with notes by F W L Thomas' *Proc. Soc. Antiq. Scot.* 10, 1872–4, 702–11; Muir, T S 1857–60 'Notice of a Beehive house in the island of St Kilda; with additional notes by Captain F W L Thomas, RN' *Proc. Soc. Antiq. Scot.*, vol 3, 225–32; Thomas, Frederick W L 1868 'On the Primitive Dwellings and hypogea of the Outer Hebrides' *Proc. Soc. Antiq. Scot.* 7, 1866–8, 153–95; Carmichael, Alexander 1941 *Carmina Gadelica* V Oliver and Boyd, Edinburgh and London, 106–11.

[56] Royal Highland and Agricultural Society of Scotland Papers.

[57] Sands 1877.

[58] MacDiarmid 1878, 232–53.

[59] The *Spectator* April 1876; The *Scotsman* February and March 1877.

[60] Sands 1877, 136.

[61] Scottish Record Office AF 57/05.

[62] Robello and Mann 1923; Jay 1925.

[63] Scottish Record Office AF 57/05, 57/06.

[64] MacKay, James A 1963 *St Kilda, Its Posts and Communications* Scottish Postmark Group, Edinburgh; MacKay, James A 1978 *Islands Postal History, No. I: Harris and St Kilda* Mackay, Dumfries.

[65] Scottish Record Office AF57 files.

[66] MacDonald personal communication, Gillies 1988, 43.

[67] Spackman, R A 1982 *Soldiers on St Kilda* Uist: Uist Community Press

[68] Scottish Record Office AF 57/27, 57/32

[69] Barry, John 1980 *Aircraft Wrecks of St Kilda*, 3–6; 19

Chapter 2

The Study of Buildings

Geoffrey Stell

At the date of the evacuation of the St Kilda archipelago in 1930, the study of Scottish vernacular and primitive building was in its infancy. Descriptions and analyses of 'ancient' structures on the archipelago had formed the subject of antiquarian enquiry, similar to those carried out elsewhere in the Western Isles and in the Highlands of the Scottish mainland.[1] This was – and remains – a fruitful area for those seeking evidence of the 'Past in the Present', a reflection of the survival of ancient practices among contemporary building customs and use.

It is also an area that has attracted Scandinavian ethnologists and folk-lorists who have sought a physical legacy of their colonising forebears in the Middle Ages, and sought to compare traditional buildings in the Northern and Western Isles of Scotland with those elsewhere in the former Norse empires.[2] In some respects, the study of the buildings of St Kilda has been a microcosm of the historiography of Scottish vernacular buildings, certainly of those within the general regional and cultural context of the Western Isles.

However, it is true to say that many of the buildings on St Kilda continued to excite an interest on the part of archaeologists greater than that among vernacular building historians. The reasons are fairly self-evident: a number of structures are of a form with which archaeologists were better able to identify, some apparently embodying ancient wheelhouse and cellular, semi-subterranean building traditions, encountered elsewhere in Early Historic and prehistoric contexts. Some lent themselves particularly well to archaeological classification, the nucleated buildings with dyked forecourts in Gleann Mór becoming known as 'horned structures' and tentatively ascribed to the Iron Age.[3]

In other ways too the buildings of St Kilda and their associated features, such as the surviving use of wall beds, stood apart. It is true that the sliding wooden

Figure 22.   Cleit in Village area showing wooden door and lock, and roped thatch, early 20th century.

tumbler-lock is not peculiar to St Kilda even though six, possibly seven, out of 22 published Scottish examples are from Hirta.[4] On the other hand, the most numerous single building-type on St Kilda, the cleit or small drystone storage building, of which there are more than 1,400 on the archipelago, has few known parallels elsewhere in Scotland or Western Britain.[5] Only the Store (1819), Church and Manse (1826), the Factor's House (*c.* 1860–70) and the 16 houses erected by the proprietor from 1861 bore a resemblance to 'improved' rural architecture of the kind familiar throughout insular and mainland Scotland. Clearly, by the 1970s the buildings of St Kilda were in need of detailed study and understanding on their own terms, both as a matter of scientific investigation and as a practical accompaniment to the programme of consolidation and restoration undertaken by The National Trust for Scotland since its assumption of the ownership of St Kilda from 1956–7.

A number of historical starting-points had long been available for this enquiry, the best-known being the descriptions by Martin Martin and the Reverend Kenneth MacAulay.[6] Less well known, but of considerable significance for an understanding of the creation of the existing settlement-pattern around Village Bay, was the account of the work done by the Reverend Neil MacKenzie, during whose ministry (1829–43) the settlement assumed its crescentic layout with a street and associated cultivation plots formed within a head dyke.[7] Even to the casual observer, it is clear that many buildings comfortably fit into this settlement framework, whilst other, and obviously older, structural remains patently do not.

Early Survey

A further key source for appreciating the impact of MacKenzie's 'improvements' in the 1830s is the plan of the Village by Sharbau, a draughtsman who carried out a survey in July 1860 and added details in 1861.[8] This cartographic witness to the changes wrought by MacKenzie provides details of some 21 or 22 houses and associated cultivation-plots, the boundaries of which are marked in schematic form. The plan, which is at a scale of 1 inch to 100 feet, also denotes the designated functions of ancillary buildings for storing corn, fish, birds and manure, and the uses of enclosed yards for cabbages and potatoes. As a result of Sharbau's later visit, the positions of two of the new houses erected in 1861 are marked, clearly overlaying existing dykes and at least one earlier structure, the beginnings of the second 19th-century housing revolution on Hirta.

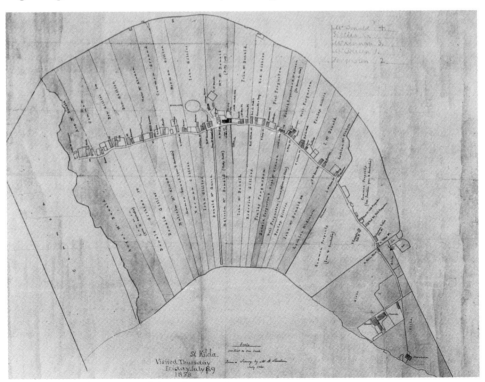

Figure 23. Sharbau's survey of the Village, 1860–1.

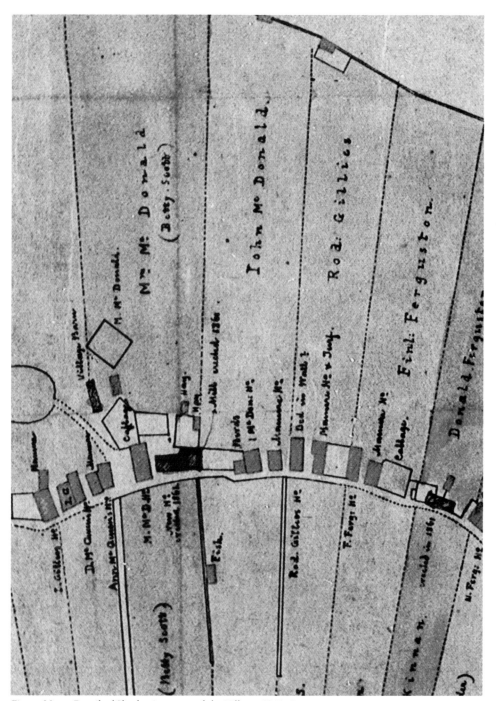

Figure 23a.   Detail of Sharbau's survey of the Village, 1860–1

Photographic Evidence

Historic photographs constitute another major source of evidence.[9] The era of photography on St Kilda began in about 1860, and photographs taken in the following decades provide a visual record of the buildings of the declining St Kildan community. Although charting the process of physical decline, these photographs show, among other things, surprising evidence of removals and reconstructions among the cleitean within and around the head dyke. Maps and drawings continued to supplement the information from photographs, but there is irony in the fact that the St Kilda group of islands only became officially recorded cartographically almost at the point of their desertion, the first Ordnance Survey map being published in 1928.[10]

Folk Memory

One indirect strand of evidence relating to population history has a bearing on the chronology and use of the buildings on the archipelago. Folk memory of the buildings on St Kilda is more confused and imprecise than is normally to be expected from Hebridean communities. One reason for this state of affairs is to be found in the smallpox epidemic of 1727 which reduced the population to 30, with only four male adults. A process of active resettlement followed, with immigrants from Harris, Uist and Skye. In the long run, this process may have been responsible for a genetic change in the male St Kildan, from being a relatively beardless to a full bearded race. It may also have dislocated continuity and tradition in other ways too, giving the buildings in Gleann Mór a greater mystery in folk memory than they might otherwise have had.[11]

Key Questions

Taken together, this body of documentary, pictorial, cartographic and ethnological evidence set an agenda of key questions to be asked of the physical, built evidence. Where, and what was the nature of the settlement and buildings prior to Reverend MacKenzie's reorganisation of the 1830s? What was the extent and nature of those changes, and to what extent were they overlaid after 1860? Where do the construction and use of the buildings of Gleann Mór fit into this chronology? And – perhaps fundamentally – how far might these questions be addressed and answered by a survey of visible remains?

Detailed Survey Begins

Various surveys of the antiquities and field monuments on the archipelago were undertaken after 1957, when The National Trust for Scotland assumed ownership of St Kilda.[12] However, the first extensive investigation to be conducted alongside a detailed historical enquiry – and the first to give as much attention to 'modern' as to the apparently 'ancient' – was that pursued by Mary Harman from 1977 onwards.[13] Her record of cleitean and other buildings throughout the archipelago and her observations of changes, not only in individual structures, but also in the overall morphology of settlement, showed that surviving visible remains embodied a rather more detailed reflection of the history of St Kilda during the past 150 years than had previously been appreciated. She also confirmed, qualified or enlarged upon previous assessments of structures which provided significant pointers or clues to earlier settlement and building practices. The desirability of further survey, analysis and synthesis was clear.

The RCAHMS Survey

Thus it was that, at the invitation of The National Trust for Scotland and in close association with Mary Harman, The Royal Commission on the Ancient and Historical Monuments of Scotland undertook a series of carefully-targeted surveys over four seasons from 1983 to 1986, the results of which were published

Figure 24.   Preparing the plane table at one of the survey stations in the Village, 1984.

in 1988.[14] For each of the four seasons the survey teams formed part of one of The National Trust for Scotland work-parties.

The survey strategy was quite simply to provide coverage, firstly, of overall areas of settlement, and, secondly, of selected individual buildings within those areas which most effectively illustrated the different phases of habitation and land use. The survey took the usual form of measured drawings, photography and a descriptive textual commentary and analysis. The key survey component in this instance was the measured survey, undertaken by teams of draughtsmen. Given the extent and complexity of the areas involved, not to mention the logistical difficulties of all operations of this kind on St Kilda, it was clear from the outset that the execution of the first of the simple strategic objectives – the area surveys – would probably be the greatest technical and physical challenge which the Royal Commission had encountered to that date, notwithstanding its considerable corporate experience of other large and difficult sites, particularly in Argyll.[15]

Ground Survey

Given also that there were constraints on the resources that RCAHMS could deploy, the target-areas for ground survey at 1:500 scale were limited to three, all on Hirta: the Village itself; the central 'bowl' of the corrie-like hollow of An Lag bho'n Tuath to the north-east of the village; and a specimen grouping of buildings and dykes in Gleann Mór, the remote valley on the north side of the island. It was recognised at the outset that, however desirable they might be, a more complete record of Gleann Mór, or of other eligible areas and building clusters, on Boreray and Soay for example, would have to remain beyond the scope of this exercise, for other survey teams to follow up.

The Village

To the casual eye, the area of the Village is conveniently defined by the existing or known line of the head dyke of the 1830s which embraces a broad arc swinging westwards from the Store to the beach at the head of Village Bay. But the remains of buildings and enclosures lay in some profusion beyond the head dyke, especially around the well, Tobar Childa, merging into, and in some cases becoming heavily disguised by, the stony lower slopes of Conachair. Many of the buildings in this area were very obviously modifications of older, usually cellular, structures. The area selected for survey thus had to take in these 'extra-mural' remains if sense were to be made of the similar but much more reduced vestiges of buildings and enclosures *within* the head dyke. The interpretation and representation of these two groups of remains tested surveying skills to a very considerable degree.

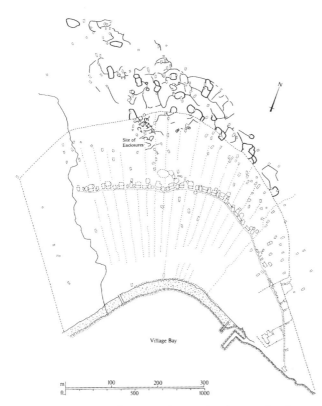

Figure 25. *Plan of Village area showing distribution of outlying enclosures and dykes.*

An Lag bho'n Tuath

As with the Village, the specific purpose behind the survey in the natural sheltered arena of An Lag bho'n Tuath was to enable an assessment of the overall pattern, purpose and the possible relationship or sequence of structures and enclosures. Some of these remains, particularly the enclosures, are comparatively well defined but An Lag lies beyond the area for which specific or circumstantial historical evidence exists, and had been a particular focus for recent field archaeological investigation.[16] Ground survey was thus a further and obvious means, among other things, of testing suggestions concerning the incidence of ridged cultivation remains and 'boat-shaped' structures of Norse or earlier origin.

Gleann Mór

Gleann Mór too has always lain beyond the historical pale, except mainly for general references to its use as a summer shieling for cattle and sheep. Remote and mysterious, the structures here have thus been the subject of even greater legend and theory from Martin Martin right down to the present day. Evidence of land use and settlement in this valley is concentrated in two main areas around the lower reaches of the Abhainn a' Ghlinne Mhóir, the densest cluster being on the well-drained eastern side of the burn where there was also a water-supply and scree material available for building. Ground survey would reveal whether there might be a general similarity in the character and relationships of buildings, dykes

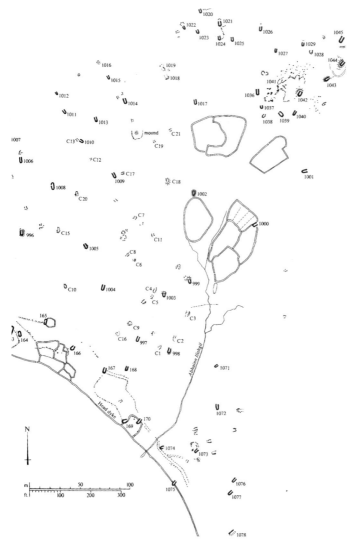

Figure 26. Distribution plan of structures in An Lag bho'n Tuath. C6 and C8 were excavated in 1993.

and enclosures here as compared to the older patterns of settlement observable in and around the Village on the other side of the island. Detailed building surveys would also be required to test the observed similarities between the nucleated and cellular structures in this area, including Taigh na Banaghaisgeich ('House of the Female Warrior' or 'Amazon's House'), and some of those surviving in the backlands of the Village. There was also a need to establish the structural and functional history of those groups of buildings variously labelled 'horned structures' or 'gathering folds',[17] some of which were overlaid with cleit-like remains.

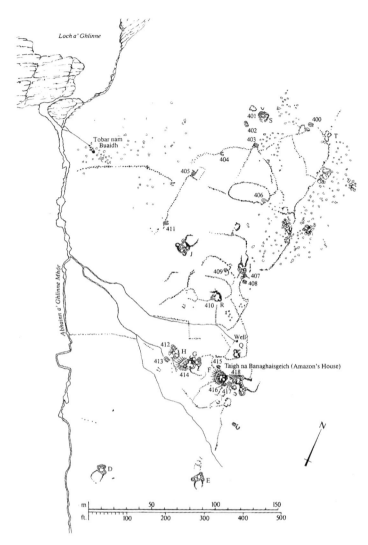

Figure 27. Nucleated buildings, dykes and enclosures in the N.E. area of Gleann Mór.

Survey Techniques

Survey techniques applied by RCAHMS to these tasks at that date consisted of a developed form of plane-table surveying, involving the use of optical (or self-reducing) alidades sighting on to calibrated poles. Such techniques, allied to the use of portable radios, had considerably extended the range of accurate area survey beyond that which had relied exclusively on traditional manual methods involving the use of measuring tapes. Even with such techniques, however, distance, topography and built obstructions, together with the need for 'infill' detail, imposed physical limits on the effective range of the instruments.

The Village area alone required the establishment of an accurate base network or grid of 14 survey stations, for the laying out of which an electronic distance measuring (EDM) instrument mounted on a theodolite was used. From each station local detail within a range of 60–70 metres was surveyed at 1:500 scale using a self-reducing alidade mounted on a plane-table board. Each area was cross-referred to its neighbouring stations on the grid. Spurs from the grid were extended into An Lag bho'n Tuath, making this by far the largest and most complex survey framework erected by RCAHMS by that date. The scale was much larger than any existing Ordnance Survey map base, and there was thus never any intention of relating it to Ordnance Survey control.

The size of the end-product was no less impressive. When conjoined, the original survey-sheets covering the Village and the adjacent area of An Lag measured some 5 metres in maximum extent. For publication purposes the detailed information contained on these sheets was brought together and reduced to a scale of 1:1250 to form a coloured and contoured pull-out, whilst a series of simplified versions of the Village plan at 1:4000 scale was used to illustrate a series of distributional points arising from the survey: early structures; remains

Figure 28. The Village showing the 1860s houses, numbers 5 to 8, with 1830s black houses between, end-on to the Street.

identifiable from the Sharbau survey; houses dating from 1861 and later; buildings built or remodelled since 1886; estate and community buildings; and outlying enclosures and dykes.

Individual Buildings

The aims and methods of survey, however, were intended to depict and interpret the buildings not only in their overall landscape and settlement context, but also, of course, in terms of their plan-form, elevation, section, structure, building materials and details. For this purpose, working at scales of 1:100 and 1:50, traditional but effective techniques of manual survey were applied, including the use of alidades, plane-tables and tapes. Notes and photographs of all buildings of interest were compiled, from which smaller groups within each area, together with a few outliers, were selected for detailed treatment in accordance with the broad aims of the strategy.[18]

In the Village, the Store and the combined Church and Schoolroom were selected to represent Estate activity. Buildings which may have embodied community functions included those which were thought to have served as a mill,

Figure 29.   Area of early settlement beyond the Village head dyke.

Figure 30.   Plane table survey of one of the nucleated buildings (Structure G) in Gleann Mór, 1985.

barn, kiln and even as a 'house' for the Village's bull. The near-standard layout and features of the 16 houses of the 1860s required only one detailed representative, but detailed surveys included almost all of those structures, mainly 'black houses', which were identifiable on the Sharbau survey or otherwise associated with the MacKenzie building programme of the 1830s. They also included all of those cleitean and cleit-like structures in the backlands which incorporated significant structural evidence of earlier design and use. Purpose-built cleitean had representative 'end-loading' and 'side-loading' types only.

Six of the most significant structures, or groups of structures, were chosen from Gleann Mór, five from the survey area and one to the south on the opposite bank of the burn, the clearest specimen of a 'gathering fold' which has not been converted out of earlier remains. The semi-subterranean 'Amazon's House' forms part of the most complex of the groups of buildings in the glen, incorporating as it does another structure of 'Amazon House' type, a 'gathering fold' and three cleitean. Below this, in a line running down the slope towards the burn, are two further groups of buildings which are only slightly less complex in character and together incorporate three cleitean remodelled out of the remains of two 'Amazon House' type structures and a 'gathering fold'. The entire line constitutes one of the most remarkable assemblages of primitive building visible anywhere in Scotland.

New Survey Techniques

Since 1986 RCAHMS, like many other bodies, has advanced through a number of further stages in the application of computer technology to its professional and business activities. In methods of landscape survey, their depiction and publication, the work on St Kilda now firmly belongs to a bygone era. There have been revolutionary changes in the sophisticated electronic collection and handling of data in the field, and in its transmission through specialised software into a range of graphic – and geographic – forms.[19] Other Hebridean islands such as Canna, where a landscape survey is in progress, stand to gain from these advances, but, even with these more powerful and efficient technical means, the ends depend just as crucially on the underlying professional expertise and rigorous effort on the part of the surveyor and interpreter.

From our present-day, thoroughly computerised, standpoint, it also seems a remarkable fact that the results of the St Kilda survey, published by HMSO as recently as 1988, were the first in RCAHMS to be prepared and presented for publication almost in their entirety in word-processed form, on a computer and with software that would now probably only find a place as a museum exhibit! The ends, too, may eventually become dated. *Buildings of St Kilda* showed how the main strands of evidence were brought together and analysed, and how a range of conclusions was reached, some definite, others requiring validation, particularly through archaeological excavation. In these and many other respects, areas of the Village, An Lag bho'n Tuath and Gleann Mór will always remain critically important research laboratories in the natural and man-made scientific field-centre that is St Kilda.

Notes and References

1 For example, Muir, T S 'Notice of a beehive house in the island of St Kilda; with additional notes by Captain F W L Thomas, RN', *Proc. Soc. Antiq. Scot.* vol 3, 1857–60, 225–32; Thomas, F W L 'On the primitive dwellings and hypogea of the Outer Hebrides' *Proc. Soc. Antiq. Scot.* vol 7, 1866–8, 153–95; and Mathieson, J 'The antiquities of the St Kilda group of islands', *Proc. Soc. Antiq. Scot.* vol 62, 1927–8, 123–32.

2 Roussell, A 1934 *Norse Building Customs in the Scottish Isles*; Campbell, A 1943–4 'Keltisk Och Nordisk Kultur I Mote Pa Hebridena' *Folkliv, Acta Ethnologia et Folkloristica Europaea*, 228–52. Some of the activities of the Swedish ethnographer, Ake Campbell, are described by Walker, B 1989 in 'Traditional Dwellings of the Uists' in *Highland Vernacular Building*, SVBWG 48–70.

3 Williamson, K 1958 in *Scottish Field*, vol 105, 46–9; Williamson, K and Boyd, J M 1960 *St Kilda Summer*, 67–75 and Cottam, M B 1979 ed Small, A *A St Kilda Handbook*, 53–61.

4 Fenton, A and Hendry, C 1984 'Wooden Tumbler Locks in Scotland and Beyond' *Review of Scottish Culture*, vol. 1, 11–28; Hay, G D 1978 'Scottish Wooden Tumbler Locks', *Post-Medieval Archaeology*, vol 12, 125–7.

5 Compare, for example, RCAHMS, 1984, *Inventory of Argyll*, vol 5, no. 131.

6 Martin, M 1698 *A Late Voyage to St Kilda*; MacAulay, K 1764 *The History of St Kilda*.

7 Mackenzie J B (ed.) 1911 *Episode in the Life of the Rev. Neil MacKenzie at St Kilda from 1829 to 1843*.

8 Royal Museum of Scotland, Society of Antiquaries of Scotland MS 158, reproduced in Stell, G P and Harman, M 1988 *Buildings of St Kilda*, 5 and rear cover.

9 Buchanan, M 1983 *St Kilda, A Photographic Album*; Stell and Harman, 1988 4–13.

10 Mathieson, J and Cockburn, A M 1928, Map of St Kilda or Hirta, scale 6 inches to 1 mile.

11 Lawson, W 1993 *Croft History: Isle of St Kilda*.

12 For example, MacGregor, D R 1960 'The Island of St Kilda' *Scottish Studies*, vol 4, 1–48; University of Keele, Department of Extra-Mural Studies (Unpublished typescript report 1966); Ordnance Survey, Archaeology Division 1967 and Cottam, M B summarised in Small, Handbook, 36–61.

13 Harman, M 1994 *The History and Culture of the St Kildans to 1930* (Unpublished PhD thesis), University of Edinburgh.

14 Stell and Harman, 1988. For an historical account of the work of RCAHMS, see Dunbar, J G 1992, 'The Royal Commission on the Ancient and Historical Monuments of Scotland, The First Eighty Years', *Transactions of the Ancient Monuments Society*, vol 36, 13–77.

15 For which, see RCAHMS, *Inventory of Argyll*, vols 1–7 1971–92.

16 Ordnance Survey, Archaeology Division, Record Card NF 19 NW18 (Davidson, J L 1967); Cottam, M B ed Small, Handbook, 39–45.

17 As described to Captain Thomas, *Proc. Soc. Antiq. Scot.*, vol 7 1870, 176.

18 Stell and Harman,1988 Descriptive List, nos 1–30.

19 For these developments, see RCAHMS, *North-east Perth, An Archaeological Landscape* (1990), *South-east Perth, An Archaeological Landscape* 1994, and the series of Afforestable Land Survey reports, notably the most recent, which relate to surveys in the Strath of Kildonan, Sutherland 1993, Glenesslin, Nithsdale 1994, and Southdean, Borders 1994.

Chapter 3

The Archaeology of St Kilda

Norman Emery and Alex Morrison

As the previous essay has demonstrated, there is a wealth of visible remains of human occupation on St Kilda, much of it not clearly understood or dated. The potential for archaeological exploration of this palimpsest has always been present, and some uncoordinated excavations took place before 1970. These have already been referred to by Mary Harman. More recent work has included survey and excavation by M. B. Cottam[1].

In the early 1980s The National Trust for Scotland held discussions with the Scottish Development Department (now Historic Scotland) on the desirability of a programme of archaeological research on St Kilda to complement the survey work undertaken by the Royal Commission. It was agreed that investigation of this unique Scottish assemblage of structures dating from prehistoric times to the early 20th century, and scheduled under the Ancient Monuments Acts, must be undertaken by skilled professional archaeologists.

Discussions followed with Professor Rosemary Cramp of Durham University. Provisional assessments of the archaeological potential of St Kilda, and of the logistics of working there, were undertaken by Dr Colleen Batey and Norman Emery on behalf of the University. As a result of their reports, an Advisory Committee was established with representatives from The National Trust for Scotland, the Royal Commission on the Ancient and Historical Monuments of Scotland, the University of Durham and Glasgow Museums.

PHASE I 1986–90

Norman Emery was appointed director of the excavation programme, and in 1986 undertook a feasibility exercise using a small core of professional archaeologists attached to National Trust for Scotland work parties. As a result, certain modifications were made to work party practices and hours for the archaeological parties, and each year three of these fortnightly groups constituted the archaeological workforce.

It was proposed to build on the survey work of the Royal Commission and attempt to answer some of the questions posed by it. Investigation would be in reverse chronological order, dealing firstly with the 19th century village settlement, and would use a number of modern scientific techniques of non-destructive survey together with excavation and environmental sampling and analysis.

The excavations carried out during the period 1986–90 were concentrated in the area of the Village Street (Figure 31). Of the most recent dwellings – the 16 houses built in the 1860s – House 6 was selected for investigation. Excavation of the interior was required before its reconstruction and refurnishing by Trust work parties. House 8 and its immediate surroundings were investigated to examine possible black house foundations identified at its east end in the Royal Commission's survey and shown on Sharbau's plan. Excavations were also carried out at black house W thought by previous observers to contain the

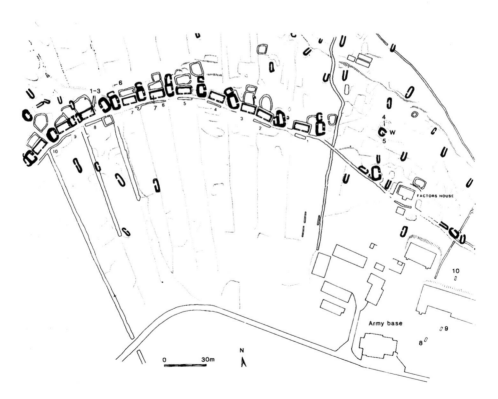

Figure 31.   Excavation areas: House 8 (areas 1–3), Black House W (areas 4–5), rubbish pit (area 6) and House 6 (area 7).

remains of a Norse or mediaeval[2] house, but identified in the Royal Commission's survey as a probable kiln barn with later alterations. This had been mentioned by several observers, but seems to have gone out of use sometime in the 19th century, and to have been lost to memory.

A rubbish pit to the rear of House 7 was also chosen to establish if these were the ash pits for viscera and other material described by Wilson in 1842. They replaced the practice of accumulating rubbish on the floors of the pre-1830s dwelling houses.

Early Settlers

The earliest evidence of settlement was found in a trench cut outside the east wall of House 8. In deposits overlying the geological formations, small fragments of coarse pottery were recovered, dated on stylistic grounds to the Bronze Age or Iron Age.

Norse Evidence

From a later stage of occupation fragments of steatite (soapstone) vessels were recovered, along with a spindle whorl of the same material from a disturbed context, and a plate-like fragment of Actinolite schist. They were recovered from the silted infill of a water channel which had run down through the site from the well Tobar Childa. The soapstone was probably quarried in Shetland, and is a material which is comparatively easy to carve. The body sherds had come from hemispherical vessels, probably used for cooking. Soapstone, once warmed, has the capacity to retain heat. The schist may be part of a baking plate and is an artefact type known from Norse sites, both in the homeland, and in the colonies.

The oval brooches found in the 19th century (page 3) are comparable with 10th century examples found elsewhere in Scotland; the excavated spindle whorl is probably late 10th to mid 11th century; the steatite vessel fragments may be classed as 'Late Norse'; while an associated pottery fragment has given a thermoluminescence date of 1135 ± 170 AD. All of this indicates that the settlement was after the Viking raiding and land seizure phase in the Northern and Western Isles, when the Hebrides were established Norse colonies.

Scottish Influence

After the Battle of Largs and the 1266 Treaty of Perth, Norse dominion in the Hebrides faded, to be replaced by Scottish influence. By the late 16th century at least, St Kilda was a MacLeod possession and by the late 17th century the islanders were living in thatched dwellings forming a 'small village', described by Martin Martin as 'carrying all the signs of an extreme poverty'. Horses were used to carry peat for fuel; cattle were kept and over-wintered in the houses; and bere barley was grown in the fields. Stone lines and primitive drains found at the House 8 site probably relate to the divisions and use of the land at that time.

The New Village

The 1830s saw the transformation of the settlement pattern on Hirta, much of it as a result of the driving force of the minister, Reverend Neil MacKenzie. The new Street line was laid out, down-slope from the earlier village; the inner cultivated land was separated from the hill grazing by a substantial stone head dyke; and changes were made to the dwellings, the layout of land plots and certain domestic practices.

At the House 8 site, excavation of the remains of a black house of this period provided useful constructional details (Figure 32). The site had been well prepared first, with an elaborate herringbone network of land drains. On this ground, substantial walls of heavy granophyre rock facings and earth core were erected, forming an elliptical structure, aligned down-slope. The building had been entered from the east long side and was divided into two. Both man and

Figure 32.   Internal features, including hearth, talan and clay floor of black house underlying house 8.

beast lived under the same roof. For drainage purposes the byre was at the bottom end and was divided from the living area by a stone wall (talan). The living area had a central hearth, in the form of a shallow stone box, where peat or turf was burnt and around it was laid a hard yellow clay floor surface. Normally the roof of these houses would be set up on the inner face of the walls, with a straw thatch cover, held down with weighted ropes.

To the west of the black house were stones representing the remains of a cleit, used as a store shed for manure. The cleitean are one of the most striking features of the landscape of St Kilda, although their form of construction and use for air drying and storage is witnessed elsewhere, particularly in the North Atlantic area, from Shetland to Greenland.

The changes to the agricultural system in the 1830s and its gradual collapse were recorded by residents and visitors to the island over the years up to evacuation. The construction of the head dyke and the layout of the plots associated with each property, divided by the consumption dykes, provide the most obvious physical indications of agricultural activity.

Excavated Agricultural Features

At Black House W, excavation of the elliptical mound at the rear of the standing structure confirmed that this had been the site of a communal corn-drying kiln (Figure 33). The structure seems to belong to this major period of change in the 1830s and because of the fire hazard was set up at some distance from the black houses. It comprised two main elements, the kiln and drying area at the top end, and a threshing and winnowing barn at the bottom. The kiln was a heavy stone construction, with a central cavity, or pot, linked to a curving flue. In the drying process a frame and cover would have been placed over the central pot, and the grain was laid on this. A fire, lit at the end of the flue, provided the heat which passed through the flue, up the pot, and circulated around the grain, drying it.

When the grain was ready, it could be taken to the lower end of the building, where the floor was a good hard yellow clay surface, suitable for threshing; the door in one wall and a hole at the opposite side, could be opened to provide the draught needed in winnowing, to remove the chaff.

The kiln had been cut into the sloping ground and it would appear that ground seepage became a problem, with several attempts to deal with it by raising the floor level of the pot. Eventually it went out of use. The lower half, the threshing barn, was converted into a tiny dwelling, while the kiln became ruinous. Later the dwelling became a byre.

Another agricultural feature was found during excavations at House 6. A soil-filled pit was located at a position marked on Sharbau's plan of the Village

Figure 33a.   Black House W, the corn-drying kiln.

Figure 33b.   Bowl of corn-drying kiln.

(1860/1861) as a cabbage plot. It may have some link with a number of small stone enclosures without entrances, which seem to be closely related to the enclosed raising beds, or planticrues, of Shetland.

The 1860s Houses

The storm of October 1860 had far-reaching effects on the islanders' lives. The damaged black houses were replaced by an alien form of dwelling – a rectangular house, of mortared stone walls, fireplaces against the end walls and a roof cover of zinc sheets on sarking boards (later replaced with tarred felt). This new accommodation, supplied by the proprietor, marked another great change, the separation of man from his animals; these new 'white houses' were purely for humans, the black houses became the byres and store-places. Stone-lined pits were cut for refuse disposal or composting and one excavated behind House 7 still retained byre litter and waste from the storage end of the black house, indicated by identifiable body fragments from a range of specific insect types, along with the plant matter.

Excavations at House 6 revealed clear evidence of the timber internal divisions of the house, with a central entrance lobby, small bedroom-store behind at the back and larger flanking living-room and bedroom. Remnants of wooden floorboards were found, and at House 8 there was a change from wood to cement, with some evidence for linoleum floor covering.

Domestic Life

The first phase of excavation resulted in the recovery and analysis of an unparalleled collection of stratified 19th and 20th century artefacts and ecofacts illustrating the nature of domestic life at that period on St Kilda.

Material culture had begun to change in the 1830s, with new furniture and fittings brought from the mainland. This process of acquiring imported goods continued until the evacuation, ousting the stone tools and coarse, hand-made pottery which had been the staple family possessions – objects which had hardly changed from those used by the earliest inhabitants. By the time of the evacuation in August 1930 the range of goods was extensive. From excavation and surface recovery the range extended from glass and crockery to furniture. Many items came from Scottish centres, particularly ports, either by direct trade or through

Figure 34. Remains of timber flooring in House 6.

45

indirect transfer via trawlers and whalers. Principal centres include Glasgow, Oban, Aberdeen and Kilmarnock, but also to a limited extent Belfast. The extent of retail distribution in Britain in the 19th century is also illustrated by the range of items which reached St Kilda from the far south of England.

Glass bottles, for instance, of particular forms or decorated with embossed lettering and designs, give some indication of the sources of these vessels and their original content (though with the proviso that the bottle may have reached the island empty, or containing a product it was not originally designed to hold).

Spirit came from Kilmarnock and Glasgow, where the majority of distilleries had been established around Port Dundas, on the northern outskirts of the new town. There is some suggestion of the presence of aqua vitae, but clearer evidence of beer bottles. Soft drinks came from Aberdeen, from Hay's works, and from Sang & Co who made Iron Brew. Bottled foods were also introduced. These included sauces from Leeds and Worcester; meat extract, in the form of Bovril, which was produced by J L Johnston in 1886; coffee essence from Glasgow; essence of rennet, a calf-stomach product used in making junket; and fruit-juice essence from Kent. Pharmaceutical products came principally from Glasgow and

Figure 35. Finds recording at the House 8 excavations.

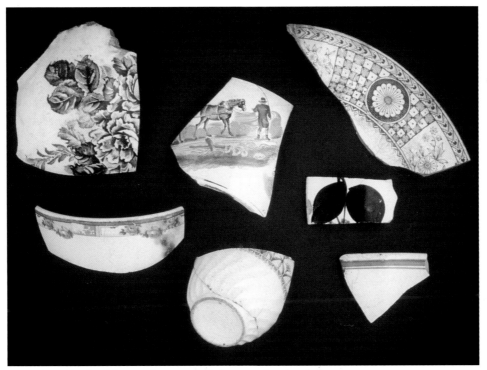

Figure 36.   Sherds of decorated pottery, including transfer-printed wares.

Oban, with embrocations (including some from Slough), for the relief of lumbago and strains; balsam and California Syrup of Figs. Lysol, a strong disinfectant manufactured in London, was also represented; and there are several examples of poison bottles, usually blue and ribbed, sometimes with embossed 'Not to be taken' warnings.

The pottery imports, which largely replaced the local coarse wares, were the cheapest on the market, and the excavated fragments came principally from bowls and plates. Amongst the stoneware pieces were sherds from items covered by the generic terms 'jam jar', 'meat loaf jar' and 'whisky jar'. There were some sherds from brown tea pots and there was even the knob from a hot water bottle. Decoration was principally sponge-printed, hand-painted or transfer-printed. Most of the material probably came over to St Kilda from the great emporium of Glasgow, but was originally derived from a variety of Scottish and English factories.

Soil conditions permitted the survival of some cloth and boot leather and a small number of clothing fasteners was recovered. The islanders had been adept at making their own clothes for centuries. In the 17th century Martin Martin referred to the belted plaid (breacan an fheilidh) and sheepskins. By the 18th and 19th centuries the distaff and wheel were in use, and cloth was either retained in its natural colours or dyed with lichen (crotal) or imported indigo. The men were the clothiers, even making the women's dresses and shifts, but by the late 19th century there was some standardisation of fashion, with the men's clothing looking similar to that worn on Harris. By the 1870s some of the woollen shirts had linen collars, and certainly linen-wool combination fabric has been found in excavation. Home tweed manufacture expanded in the mid-19th century to become an income-generating product, both for export and for tourist sales, as did knitted goods. Imports added to the islanders' 'wardrobe', included shawls, coloured petticoats, and 'Turkey red' handkerchiefs, probably dyed in Glasgow. Imported fasteners found in excavation included a buckle from Paris, a trouser fastener patented by a Baltimore manufacturer, and papier mâché and mother-of-pearl buttons (possibly made in Birmingham).

The leather found in excavation came from inexpensive workwear boots and shoes produced in mainland factories. Examples included rivetted types with laced fronts, but there was evidence of wear marks and patching. From several of the excavated sites leather offcuts and scraps were found, indicating some local expertise in cobbling – a case of make do and mend, whereas in earlier centuries the islanders had been capable of tanning leather and making their own basic shoes.

Outside influences also impinged on the home. Not only was the house design an import, but many of the furnishings and fittings came from the mainland. The excavated artefacts include standard Imperial wainscotting, bedsteads, fittings for dressers, picture-frame glass, and Birmingham-made paraffin lamps.

The first phase of excavation has resulted in the publication by The National Trust for Scotland and HMSO of Norman Emery's monograph *The Archaeology of St Kilda* 1995. The National Trust for Scotland has deposited the finds from the excavation in Glasgow Museums to join its collection of St Kilda material there.

PHASE II 1991-5

Durham University's involvement with St Kilda ended in 1990 and Glasgow University became the centre for archaeological research on St Kilda. Dr Alex Morrison of Glasgow University was appointed Director of Excavations for Phase II, working in association with Paul Johnson (Ruaival), Tony Pollard (An Lag bho'n Tuath) and Jacqui Huntley (soils and palaeobotany).

Phase II brought with it a shift in emphasis from excavation to survey work and a period of re-assessment. It was decided to concentrate on testing techniques new

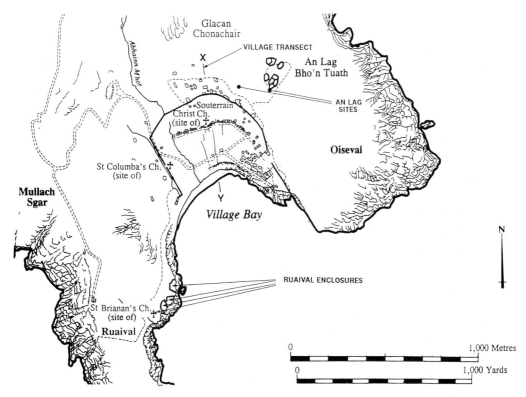

Figure 37. Locations of post-1990 fieldwork on Hirta.

to St Kilda. These included geophysical survey using a resistivity meter whose readings were fed into a portable computer and processed on site, transect survey and sampling for geochemical analysis.

Following on the work of the RCAHMS in the 1980s, the 1991–2 programme produced a plane table survey of part of the An Lag bho'n Tuath area indicating that the visible drystone enclosures overlay earlier settlement features. Geophysical and optical survey on Ruaival showed traces of older terrace platforms, field enclosures and possibly earlier building foundations.

A Transect through the Village

Excavation in 1992 was aimed at analysing an area which would take in the Village and hopefully the immediate pre-Village period. A 10 metre wide strip or transect was laid out to run from above the head dyke down to the beach (Figure 37). Its central line ran from a point *c.* 12 metres to the west of the southern gable end of cleit no 151. Its western boundary follows the remains of a field wall which contains cleitean no 59 and no 67, cuts through the eastern part of the burial ground, along the eastern side of black house O on the Street, and continues

Figure 38.
Taking soil samples along a transect across the terraces at Ruaival.

down the field wall past cleit no 85, ending above the beach. The eastern boundary follows the remains of the field wall delineating the eastern limit of the same land strip, passing along the western side of cleit no 80, to the back wall of House no 10 of the 1860s on the Street and continuing down to the beach along the eastern side of the largest consumption dyke in the Village, with cleitean no 91 and no 92 at the southern end. The land holding bisected and bounded by these lines is that shown as belonging to John Gillies in Sharbau's plan of 1860-61 to the north of the Street and to John Gillies and Donald McQueen to the south of the Street. This strip was chosen for the transect because it takes in the medieval well, Tobar Childa, the 'Bull's House', Calum Mór's house and part of the area of early settlement above the head dyke as well as samples of enclosures, cleitean and later settlement.

Along the central line and on either side a vegetation survey was carried out. Soil samples were taken at 5 metre intervals along the central and both side boundaries (for phosphate analysis, magnetic susceptibility measurement and pH measurement), a geophysical survey was attempted and the strip was levelled at 1 metre intervals. Results are still being evaluated, but it is interesting to note the changes in phosphate levels in the region between the head dyke and the Street lower down the slope – an area on which pre- and post-1830s agriculture would have been concentrated.

Ruaival

In 1992, at Ruaival, to the south-west of the Village, survey work which was started in the previous year was completed. There are four drystone-built enclosures here, three of which are open to the edge of the sea-cliff, suggesting that they were not intended to enclose animals! Enclosure 4, the farthest south-west, is shown by OS maps to be the location of the 'chappel' of St Brianan, as mentioned by Martin Martin, but there is no evidence on the ground to suggest such a structure. More important are the older turf-covered remains of terraces, platforms and sub-rectangular foundations of an earlier occupation and use of the site which underlie the drystone enclosures and are exceptionally clear in enclosure 1, less so in the others (Figure 39). In 1991, geophysical (electrical resistivity) survey of these turf-covered foundations of terraces or platforms most clearly visible in enclosure 1 showed that they were not of stone construction and could have been made of turf. Their long axes in general run down the slope, not

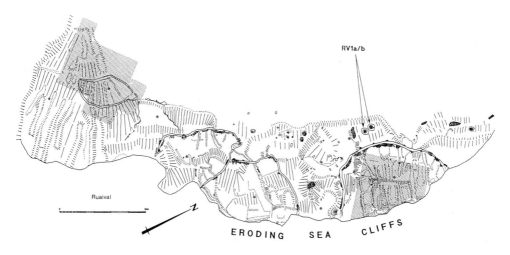

Figure 39.   Enclosures and other remains on Ruaival. Shaded areas show location of geophysical survey.

across it, and there are distinct gaps between 'platforms'. If these are the remains of habitations, then their form and possible turf-structure can be paralleled elsewhere in Scotland. They may, however represent agricultural activity rather than dwellings, although their size is more suggestive of garden than field, but they are not orientated to make best use of the slope in terms of possible drainage, erosion, etc.

Soil samples were taken from transects along the centre lines of two of the platforms situated within enclosure 1, one platform in enclosure 2 and one platform in enclosure 3. The chemical and physical analysis of the samples could indicate the presence of hearths or byre areas within the platforms, but if such features are consistently absent then an agricultural or horticultural function might be possible. They are similar to surface features associated with the drystone enclosures on An Lag bho'n Tuath (page 57).

Outside and possibly associated with these platforms/terraces are some ruinous circular and sub-circular foundations which were most clearly visible to the west of and upslope from enclosure 1. Similar and possibly similar structures are located between enclosures 1 and 2. Noted in 1992, these could have had either a storage or a dwelling function. If the platforms/terraces are agricultural then it could be that the circular/sub-circular structures were the habitations of those responsible for the agricultural or 'horticultural' activity, although they appear to be of very small size. They are not unlike shieling bothy foundations, but it seems unlikely that they could be either cleitean or bothies associated with the Village area. They are architecturally very different from cleitean or their remains and there would appear to be no logical reason for the construction of bothies on a site at a similar elevation and within 15 minutes walk of a contemporary village settlement. They are almost certainly associated with the turf-covered remains lying within and running beneath the more recent drystone enclosures, and the only cleit in the vicinity is built into these drystone walls. Soil samples were taken from the interiors of three of the circular structures and control samples from outside in an attempt to determine possible function.

The turf-covered remains of what must have been the enclosing wall of these early structures runs along the present edge of the cliff, surviving as a slight 'lip' at the cliff edge where it is being eroded away. This is a discrete area of high archaeological potential, spatially (and possibly chronologically) detached from the main Village area. The circular and sub-circular structures suggest a different technique and style of building from that of the Village. The stones used, visible in a number of areas where erosion has occurred, are noticeably smaller. This could of course be explained by the nature of the raw material available from the neighbouring scree slopes, or the robbing and re-use of the larger stones elsewhere, but it could represent a different building tradition where turf was the main structural material with a fill or cladding of smaller stones. Most of what can be seen of the surviving remains, and certainly the circular features, differs substantially from the architecture of the cleitean and some other Village structures. Some attempt at levelling may have been made, since there are traces of several scoop-like hollows in the vicinity.

In 1993 an excavation trench was established over two of the apparently circular/sub-circular stone scatters (designated RV1a and RV1b), situated just to the west of the most northerly of the four extant drystone enclosures (enclosure 1). The earlier part of the work consisted of deturfing the area around the circles; the turf was never more than about 5 centimetres in thickness. The circles have walls which have spread and tumbled beyond their original thickness and there were hardly any traces of an inner or an outer face. RV1b, the more northerly structure, appeared to have a low course of stones running across the arc of the circle internally. Under the turf cover, where such existed, the loose stones were located in a matrix of turf-soil with masses of roots. This material seems to have worked its way right down through most of the covering stones. Below this the

Figure 40.   Two cell-like stone structures on Ruaival before excavation.

stones were embedded in a sticky brown earth matrix. At a lower level in RV1b, patches of what at first were thought to be charcoal or burnt peat proved to be manganese. In the time available, it was not possible to excavate completely the interior of either circle.

In summary, the excavations so far suggest that the circular/sub-circular sites were of coarse rubble construction, much of the material of which had collapsed into and downhill of the structures. After removal of the collapse, both structures were seen to contain remnants of walling, possibly only an inner face, very faint, delimiting a sub-circular central 'activity' area. In the most northerly of the two structures (RV1B), the outlines of what appear to be traces of an 'entrance passage' were beginning to emerge at the close of the first season. No material that would provide undoubted chronological or cultural indicators was recovered, but some fragments of what appear to be rudimentary bowls or mortars were found.

An Lag bho'n Tuath

The evidence for human activity in this area to the north north east of the Village seems fairly clear to the eye. At first sight, the corrie is dominated by the four large drystone built enclosures. These are higher and more massive than the enclosures at Ruaival, with very large orthostatic stones as foundations; the walls have been kept in a good state of repair. A closer look reveals remains scattered across the corrie area, in some cases running up to, and inside, the walls of the more recent enclosures (Figure 41). It was felt that this group of sites might yield information on the earlier, possibly prehistoric, chronology of Hirta.

A plane table survey of the area was completed in 1992. This was intended to show in detail the four drystone enclosures and a series of low ridges and banks which appear within and under these enclosures and at the foot of the slopes of the Gap and Oiseval. Some of these are probably fluvio-glacial features but many are of linear or rectangular form and show a degree of uniformity in size and orientation such that they could represent features associated with cultivation.[3]

In many cases the features run under and exist within the confines of the walls of the four enclosures, suggesting a change of land use through time. Other features detected during the survey have left 'negative' traces – ie they resemble platforms or scarps cut into the earth, which may simply represent the removal of turf for use as roofing material or fuel, but some could also be small enclosures or platforms. At least one, possibly two, elongated platform features were recorded; these were about 14–15 metres long and had rounded ends. One of these lies just outside enclosure 1 to its south-east, with its northern end possibly located beneath the enclosure wall (see below). In 1992 it was thought that these features

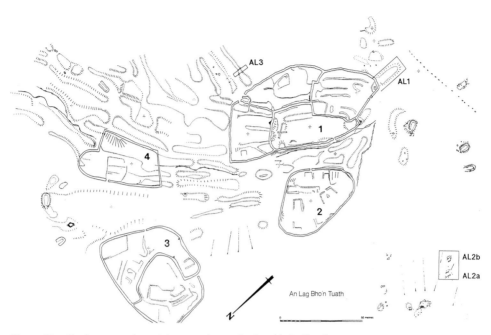

Figure 41.   Enclosures and surviving remains on An Lag bho'n Tuath.

might represent the remains of former structures resembling long houses, but probing with the auger did not reveal any obvious stones related to the structure nor was charcoal detected.

Another series of sites was identified around the southern lip of the corrie and across its eastern side towards the lower slopes of Glacan Chonachair. These differed from those previously described in that their main structural material appeared to be stone rather than earth. They included several small cairn-like structures as well as the 'boat-shaped' features mentioned above and described and excavated by Cottam.[4] The remains of what seems to be a badly robbed and denuded field dyke, now represented by a line of earth-fast stones, was traced for part of the way across the lip of the corrie. A number of soil samples were taken within the enclosures and from other features in the corrie.

Two major areas of the corrie were selected for investigation in 1993. The first excavation concentrated on a pair of stone settings recorded by earlier surveys. These were designated AL2a and b (C8 and C6 respectively on the plan of Stell and Harman[5]). These features, formerly termed 'boat-shapes', appear to represent the central settings of sub-circular cairns. The sites had a shallow covering of

Figure 42.   Removing heavy stones during excavation of 'boat-shaped' settings on An Lag bho'n Tuath.

grass, sphagnum moss, heather and peaty soil – the whole acting like a sponge for the ground water in this area. With several days rain the corrie becomes a great saucer holding a mass of water which constantly floods the sites. On stripping the covering material, a series of kerbs became visible within the larger of the two cairns (AL2a), which lay immediately to the north west of its neighbour (AL2b). The two cairns appear to be joined, or at least the stone matrix, robbed cairn or 'platform' which surrounds them appears to be continuous, and it is possible that the more substantial of the two (AL2a) was constructed later, perhaps including material taken from the earlier structure. In the central area of the larger cairn were traces of various pits and cuts, some of which appeared to run beneath the stone setting and cairn. No finds were recovered from the central area, but several coarse stone tools, including what may be ard tips, were recovered from the matrix of the smaller cairn. The sites were not completely excavated in this first season. These cairns and stone settings may represent funerary monuments but further excavation will be required before such an interpretation can be verified.

A long sub-rectangular 'tongue' of higher land or earth platform, designated AL1, was also investigated. As mentioned above, one end (about one-third) of

Figure 43. Excavation of stone settings on An Lag bho'n Tuath.

this feature lies inside and underlies the wall of Enclosure 1. It has a raised edge or 'lip' running around the edge of the flat top, and it is not unlike the rectangular and sub-rectangular turf-covered foundations near the edge of the cliff at at Ruaival. It was initially thought that this feature might be the turf-covered foundation of a structure but excavation and soil sampling suggests more an artificial bed of earth, possibly used for some type of cultivation if the soil were sufficiently organic. A grass/sphagnum surface overlies about 30 centimetres of immature, peaty soil; below this is a layer of black/brown loamy soil with many grits ('friable loam with abundant grits') overlying a foundation level of large blocky stones resting in and on an ochreous-red gritty clayey material. Soil profiles were taken across this feature and a number of soil samples were removed for phosphate and other analysis.

Pollen sampling and soil analysis of another of these structures has yielded evidence of arable weeds and plants which do not exist in the vicinity today and some of the grass pollen grains are large enough to suggest barley, but this requires further analysis. Excavation of another of these areas in 1994 showed definite tip lines in the soil profile and uncovered a large rim sherd of black ware pottery from a location well below the surface, confirming the human association. A preliminary examination of the sherd suggests similarities with pottery from the excavations of the black house in the Village Street. The question as to whether the pottery had been used *in situ* or been dumped here with earth from elsewhere remains to be answered.

The work on these platforms and terraces has thus moved nearer to confirming their use as growing areas (or possibly a St Kildan form of the lazy bed) for root crops or perhaps even some kind of grain crop. Their structure shows a very great depth of usable soil in the central saucer-like area of the corrie and implies a great amount of careful work on the part of the St Kildans at some time in the past. Their use had already been suggested by Williamson and Boyd[6] where they write that: 'It is possible that the wide and irregular cultivation ridges on the floor of the corrie . . . belonged to [the] mediaeval settlement. At a later date, probably about 1830, a number of curiously shaped enclosures were erected there to protect the root crops either from wind or grazing stock, or both.' This is also noted by Stell and Harman[7] in their description of the dry-stone enclosures: 'Although generally interpreted as sheep stells, their walls, vertically-faced externally and battered

Figure 44.   *Excavation of earthen terraces or 'lazy beds' on An Lag bho'n Tuath.*

internally, appear to have been constructed to exclude rather than contain livestock'. . . . 'An Lag is a naturally sheltered area, and these enclosures may have arisen in an attempt, perhaps in the 1830s, to enclose suitable land for growing vegetables.' This does not rule out the possibility, as suggested by Williamson and Boyd, that the earthen platforms were used by even earlier groups from the medieval village. This has implications for Ruaival as well. None of the platforms and terraces within and underlying the ruinous stone enclosures there have yet been excavated, but in shape and height they resemble very closely those on An Lag bho'n Tuath and may have fulfilled the same function at a similar time.

Notes and References

[1] Cottam, M B 1979 'Archaeology' ed Small, A *St Kilda Handbook*, National Trust for Scotland, Edinburgh, 36–61.

[2] Williamson, K and Boyd, J M 1960 *St Kilda Summer,* Hutchison, London.

[3] Stell, Geoffrey P and Harman, Mary 1988 *Buildings of St Kilda*, RCAHMS, Edinburgh.

[4] Cottam 1979.

[5] Stell and Harman 1988.

[6] Williamson and Boyd 1960, 58.

[7] Stell and Harman 1988, 23.

Chapter 4

Bird and Marine Life

Mark Tasker

The St Kilda archipelago is arguably Europe's most important seabird colony. The cliffs and stacs provide innumerable sites for nesting, and the rich, productive waters around the islands support a good supply of food. The association between St Kilda and its human population has also to a great extent relied on the sea. The most famous use of marine resources was the great bird hunts of earlier centuries. In 1875, the export of 566 gallons of fulmar oil, 2,103 lb of black feathers and 1,675 lb of grey feathers[1] would have demanded a large harvest of seabirds; additionally, feathers and oil were used on the island itself. A harvest in the region of 10,000 fulmars would be needed for this amount of oil. Sands[2] calculated that 89,600 puffins were killed in 1876. This use of birds was an indirect way of using the sea's resources.

Fish were not caught commercially by the St Kildans until the late 19th century, and even then the quantities were relatively small. Nevertheless, fish were exported and were of value to the islands in the late 19th century. Fishing was carried out both from the rocks and from small boats. The relative importance of these activities may be seen in the descriptions of the menfolk of St Kilda in the 1861 census: the heads of households were referred to as 'cottar and cragsman', the sons as 'cragsman and fisherman' and younger sons as 'fowlers'.

Fishing still continues in the seas around the islands, but now it is carried out by ships from far away. Fishing vessels from many parts of Europe use St Kilda's waters; a fleet of French trawlers may commonly be found north and west of St Kilda fishing for saithe. Spanish vessels fish for ling. In the summer, lobsters and crabs are fished by creel boats from England, with the catch being exported live to the Continent from Scottish ports. Village Bay is used for shelter during poor weather.

Present-day inhabitants of the island no longer exploit the birds and marine

Figure 45.   A German stern trawler fishes the waters within five miles of St Kilda.

life, but instead study it. The aim of this chapter is to examine some of the most frequently posed questions about St Kilda's bird and marine life, and to tell a little of the way these questions are answered.

Bird Counts

One of the most frequently asked questions is 'How many birds are there?' Early visitors to the islands spoke of innumerable birds and skies blackened with flying puffins. It was not until after the evacuation that any systematic counts started. Harrisson and Lack[3] counted the gannets and resident landbirds in 1931, and there have been several counts since, summarised by Harris and Murray[4] and Tasker.[5] Figure 46 indicates the most recent population estimates for St Kilda. The last full count of most species was in 1987 (except gannet, 1985), but some species on some parts of the archipelago have been counted since by Walsh and Tasker in counts held on the Joint Nature Conservation Committee/Seabird Group Seabird Colony Register.

The giant cliffs and exposed location of St Kilda do not allow counts to be made easily. On Hirta and Dùn, it is possible to find suitable vantage points to

Species	Unit	Island								Total
		Hirta	Dùn	Soay	Soay Sound stacs	Levenish	Boreray	Stac Lee	Stac an Armin	
Fulmar	aos	35349	12018	5679	432	80	6802	39	2387	62786
Manx shearwater	p/a	p	p	?	0	0	?	0	?	?
Storm Petrel	p/a	p	p	?	0	?	p	0	?	?
Leach's Petrel	p/a	p	p	?	0	?	p	0	?	?
Gannet (1985)	nests	0	0	0	0	0	24676	13521	11853	50050
Shag	nests	25	21	4	0	0	2	0	0	52
Great Skua	aot	44	0	8	0	0	2	0	0	54
Lesser Black-Backed Gull	aot	129	13	0	0	0	12	0	0	154
Herring Gull	aot	14	4	0	0	3	38	0	0	59
Great Black-Backed Gull	aot	13	12	5	0	10	15	0	1	56
Kittiwake	aos	1719	1231	1306	79	0	2923	245	326	7829
Guillemot	Indivs	10465	2648	2219	1742	26	3679	490	1436	22705
Razorbill	indivs	1221	1809	263	8	9	252	15	237	3814
Black-Guilemot	indivs	0	10	2	0	0	5	0	0	17
Puffin	ob	10800	27300	39500	1	0	63000	0	100	140701

aos= apparently occupied sites; p/a=presence/absence; aot=apparently occupied territories;
indivs=individuals; ob=occupied burrows

Updated from Tasker *et al.* (1987), using mostly uinpublished infformation from the JNCC/Seabird Group Seabird Colony Register

Figure 46.   Most recent estimates of total number of seabirds on islands and stacs of St Kilda.

enable most of the birds on cliffs to be counted using telescopes. Some of these vantage points require a safety rope, and biologists need a particularly good head for heights in the airiest locations. Counts need to be conducted without too much wind (which causes telescopes to shake, and under the worst conditions may lower the numbers of birds on the cliffs). Good visibility is also needed as some sites being counted may be 1 kilometre away. Add to this the fact that the standard method for some species requires counts to be made in a limited number of hours during the first three weeks of June, and it becomes obvious why the birds are not counted completely more often than once every ten to fifteen years.

Some parts of the cliffs of Hirta are invisible from the land, and these need to be viewed from a boat. Looking up at the 450 metre cliff of Conachair from below from the deck on a gently rolling trawler, and being asked to count the fulmars is an intimidating experience. Similarly, most of the birds nesting low on the cliffs of Boreray and the Stacs are best counted from the sea, with some checks possible from vantage points on Boreray and Stac an Armin. Gannets nest higher on the cliffs; counts of this species are carried out from photographs, taken from the land, sea and air. Some checking on the ground is advisable. Despite the relatively regular spacing of nests within a gannetry, counting from photographs is not straightforward. Photographs are frequently not taken from the perfect angle, or some nest sites are partially hidden by the ground. Nevertheless, counts within 3% or 4% of the mean were made by three independent counters of photographs of Stac an Armin.[6]

Burrow-nesting birds present entirely different problems. Four seabird species nesting on St Kilda nest exclusively in burrows – Manx shearwater, storm petrel, Leach's petrel and puffin. Numbers of the first three species are not known; even their distribution on St Kilda is uncertain. The only way of detecting these species is to visit suitable nesting habitats by night, and listen for their calls from their burrows. Most of the easily accessible parts of Hirta, Dùn and Boreray have been visited by night. On Hirta and Boreray, storm petrels were found in the drier rock ridges and in walls and cleitean built on dry ground. Leach's petrels were more commonly found in burrows on the steeper slopes. Away from St Kilda, tapes played by day outside burrows have elicited calls from incubating birds underground, which enables occupied burrows to be counted. This technique has yet to be tried systematically on St Kilda.

Figure 47.   Biologists working on the slope of Dùn, counting puffin burrows within fixed quadrats.

The number of puffins on St Kilda has long been a matter for conjecture and debate. There was no doubt that St Kilda held the largest concentration of puffins in the British Isles. The large colonies on Dùn, Soay and Boreray occupy wide areas of ground on steep slopes. Dùn is relatively accessible, and in the early 1970s, Mike Harris established a series of transects running across the colony. These were replaced in 1977 with a series of randomly-placed permanently-marked quadrats within the colony.[7] Random quadrats can be used to represent the whole colony statistically. During puffin incubation, all holes are explored within the quadrat. A burrow in use frequently has fresh diggings or droppings at its entrance, but if this evidence is not visible, it is necessary to feel down the burrow. If the end cannot be reached with a bare arm, short lengths of bamboo can be helpful. Careful exploration often either leads to a nip from the beak of the incubating bird, or a brief touch of the egg. The numbers of occupied burrows are recorded for each quadrat, and extrapolated eventually to the whole colony area. This technique has revealed that about 42,000 burrows on Dùn are presently occupied. In 1986 a similar technique was applied on Boreray, which indicated that about 63,000 burrows were present, and in 1987, the much more inaccessible island of Soay was tackled.

Figure 48. The warden dive-bombed by a great skua while marking a nest.

Ground-nesting birds are relatively easy to census by searching areas systematically for nests. The greatest problem is the aggressiveness of the great skuas. These birds swoop to attack intruders on their territory, and in recent years one or two pairs on Mullach Mór have even managed to knock over researchers visiting their nests. Usually such attacks can be warded off by holding a stick overhead.

Changes in Bird Numbers

Having established how many birds are present, the next most frequent question is 'Are the numbers changing?' Similar counting techniques can be employed for those species whose numbers are already reasonably well known. Gannets have been counted in much the same way since 1959, and there was only a very slight increase between then and 1985. Extrapolations of seven counts of puffins on Dùn between 1975 and 1987 averaged 36,500, with all seven estimates being within 11,000 of this figure. There seems to have been a trend of decreasing numbers early in this period, with an unsteady gain since. It is impossible to judge claims of major decreases in numbers in the past on Dùn.

Plots to record the changes in numbers of the cliff-nesting species on Hirta were established by Paul Walsh in 1990. These were placed randomly in order to allow changes in the visible part of the colony to be estimated in the future. Counts of these sites made in 1993 revealed that there has been no significant change in the numbers of guillemots, razorbills and kittiwakes present, but that fulmar numbers had declined by around 9%. These plots will be re-counted at three yearly intervals. Numbers of great skua territories have also been counted regularly, and have shown a steady increase from the first breeding record on Hirta in 1963. Overall, the counts indicate that most of the populations of seabirds on St Kilda are either similar to those of the 1970s or have increased.

One problem with such counts comes in interpreting their meaning. Seabirds tend to live relatively long lives once they reach adulthood, but have a long period of immaturity (around ten years in the case of fulmar). Individuals of some species do not breed if feeding conditions are adverse in that year. There can thus be large fluctuations in numbers of birds attempting to breed in any one year, without a similar fluctuation in the overall population. If seabird monitoring is an indirect way of looking at the quality of the seas around St Kilda, then counting numbers present in any one year may not be a great help. Any general change could be buffered by immatures starting to breed earlier than normal, or might be exaggerated by much of the colony taking a year off breeding. Such monitoring would not be very helpful in pointing at the part of the life cycle of the seabirds where there has been change. The quality of the seas around St Kilda for seabirds is better monitored by looking at breeding success in any one year. In a 'good' year, more young would be produced per breeding attempt than in a 'bad' year. This is easier to measure, and more sensitive in those species that can produce more than one young per year. Breeding success of a guillemot pair is either one or none; that of a kittiwake pair can be none, one, two or three.

A scheme for carrying out this monitoring has now been established on St Kilda. The scheme is part of a wider programme which monitors similar parameters at colonies scattered around the coasts of Britain and Ireland. St Kilda is one of the key stations in this chain. An indication of whether variation in breeding performance is local or widespread may be obtained by comparing results from St Kilda with those from elsewhere. Breeding performance may vary for a number of reasons. The most obvious is through variations in food supply, but excessive predation or disturbance can also reduce success. Poor weather during critical phases of breeding can have adverse effects both directly through, for instance, flooding of burrows, and indirectly through alteration of feeding conditions. Any results therefore need careful interpretation.

What the Birds Eat

It is obviously important to study the diet of birds. The easiest opportunity to do this is to examine the diet of young on the nest, or of adults returning to their young. The diet of fulmars was examined by Furness and Todd.[8] Around 9% of the young and adult fulmars which they handled regurgitated food when handled for ringing and measuring. Over 70% of samples examined held zooplankton; the euphausiid *Meganyctiphanes norvegica* and the mysid *Gnathophausia zoea* were found most frequently among a variety of species taken. Both of these species of zooplankton are commonest at the water's surface by night, suggesting that fulmars feed frequently by night. As this regurgitated food is oily and semi-digested, researchers have a good idea of smells that native St Kildans must have been accustomed to: clothes used during fulmar ringing are not welcomed in accommodation areas! Furness and Todd[9] compared the diet of fulmars on St Kilda with that on Foula in Shetland. Foulan birds consumed a much higher proportion of sandeels. Furness and Todd[10] considered that this was a factor that allowed the higher breeding success and adult survival rate that fulmars achieved on Foula compared with St Kilda.

Mike Harris and his co-workers have looked at the species composition of fish caught by puffins on St Kilda. The easiest way to examine this is to net adult puffins returning to their burrows. Puffins carry food for their chick in their beak, and on colliding with the net, release their load. It is relatively easy to gather this load from the ground, and determine its make-up. Harris and Hislop[11] showed

Figure 49.   A fulmar glides over Stac A'Langa.

that diet was variable from day to day, and between years. In the early 1970s, rockling, sandeels and sprat dominated the diet. Puffin chicks grew best in the year when sprat was the most important dietary component, and least well when whiting were important.

Individuals of two species of seabird on St Kilda, great black-backed gull and great skua, feed on other seabirds. Great black-backed gulls have been studied by Mike Harris[12] and Kenny Taylor[13] when they feed on puffins. Individual birds specialise in attacking the large wheels of flying puffins that occur above colonies. Once the gulls have caught a bird, they usually take it to a feeding area (which frequently has a pool of water) and kill it, then, by shaking, turn the skin inside out and consume the bird. The researcher can check and count these eviscerated skins, though this frequently means abseiling down to the feeding area. Mike Harris found 5,500 full-grown puffins killed during a four-year study on Dùn. Like the native St Kildan the researcher on St Kilda may also need to be a cragsman.

Feeding Areas

Another question asked of researchers on St Kilda is 'Where are birds feeding?' This is obviously important if we are to understand the interaction of seabirds with their marine environment. Threats to birds, such as oil pollution, occur primarily while the birds are at sea. In order to answer this question, the modern St Kildan needs to go to sea. In June 1987 and 1989, the Seabirds at Sea Team of the (then) Nature Conservancy Council visited St Kilda in the breeding season on board a chartered survey vessel. Individual birds cannot be followed out to sea with a survey vessel (although this might be possible using radio or satellite tags attached to birds). However, St Kilda is in a sufficiently isolated position that birds sighted relatively near the islands are likely to come from its colonies. Instead, the research ship can be used at sea to survey a sample of the population as a whole. A standard technique has been evolved that estimates densities of birds in the area surveyed. Researchers sit or stand high on the research vessel, with as clear a view as possible of the strip of water beside the track of the boat. All birds occurring in this strip of water are counted. Observations of the behaviour of birds, their flight direction and other features are logged. Frequently, due to the wind and waves, this can be a cold and wet task. If these survey results

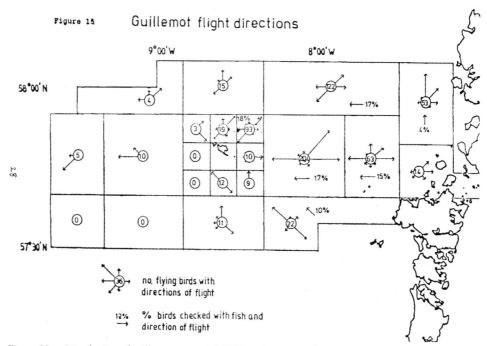

Figure 50. *Distribution of guillemots around St Kilda in June 1986 (from Leaper et al. 1988). On the basis of recorded flight directions, the high densities of birds recorded near Harris are probably of birds other than from St Kilda. Almost all of the birds seen west of St Kilda were in flight.*

are plotted on a map, a great deal of information on the use made of an area by birds can be inferred.

During the 1987 survey, Leaper *et al.*[14] found that guillemots and razorbills were found almost exclusively close to and to the east of St Kilda. Puffins were more widespread but again, higher densities were found to the east. A much higher proportion of the razorbill population fed within 10 kilometres of the islands compared to the other two species of auk. Maximum feeding ranges for auks from St Kilda were estimated by recording how far from the island birds were seen carrying fish in its direction. Ranges of 55 kilometres, 38 kilometres and 40 kilometres were recorded for guillemot, razorbill and puffin respectively. Guillemots were found to be feeding almost exclusively in waters less than 80 metres in depth. Those feeding towards Harris, over the Whale Rock Bank, were feeding on sandeels, while those feeding near to the islands themselves were catching small cod-like fish, particularly Norway pout. There have been no local surveys of numbers of sandeel, but it seems likely that the sandy conditions in relatively shallow water on the Whale Rock Bank are good for sandeels, and therefore for those birds that prey on them.

Storm petrels and fulmars were found mostly at or beyond the edge of the continental shelf to the west of the islands, and Leach's petrels were only seen beyond this boundary. Large flocks of fulmars were often associated with fishing vessels. However, densities near to the continental shelf edge were high, even discounting birds obviously associated with fishing vessels. This may seem to contradict the findings from Furness and Todd looking at the diet of birds caught on land, but it is likely that this shelf edge area is also the most important for zooplankton coming to the surface by night.

Marine Life

The modern St Kildan has also begun to ask about marine life other than birds around the islands. In contrast to earlier days, underwater breathing apparatus has revolutionised capabilities and it is now possible to descend underwater to explore areas below the waves. The clarity of the water, and St Kilda's remote and unique location, has made the archipelago very attractive to visiting divers. St Kilda's remoteness poses difficulties. Divers must be self-sufficient and work from ocean-going vessels with on-board compressors. St Kilda's shores are very exposed to wave action, and any life here has to be able to cling on and survive the fiercest of Atlantic storms. Around most of the group, the cliffs continue underwater to depths of 40 or 50 metres, with boulders at the base. In some areas, movement of these rocks, presumably during winter storms, has kept the bedrock clear of most marine growth at depths as great as 50 metres. There is little

Figure 51. Diver at underwater cliff, Scarbh Stac with plumose anemones, soft corals and kelp.

sediment in the area. The sandy beach in Village Bay is present only in summer. In winter the sand is washed back into the bay itself, which has a sandy seabed throughout the year, inhabited by octopus, cuttlefish, flat fish and thick-shelled bivalves.

Wave action has also exploited local geological weakness to form caves and geos. Such erosion is still in progress, albeit slowly, at sea level, but was also happening in the past, when sea levels were lower. The lowest 'erosional surface' is around 120 metres below present sea level, and was probably produced during the last major northern hemisphere glaciation period some 18,000 years ago. A more complex surface about 40 metres below sea level was probably formed between 10,000 and 11,000 years ago.[15] These now submerged gullies, tunnels, caves and arches are one of the most characteristic features of the underwater scenery of St Kilda.[16] Underwater researchers consider the marine life of the cave system to be among the finest in Britain. These cave marine communities are able to survive the surge of waves, and in headland areas, relatively strong tidal currents. Surveys of underwater life around St Kilda have concentrated on systematic recording of underwater habitats, together with still and video photography.[17] Specimens have also been preserved for identification by experts.

Conservation

In a similar fashion to their forebears, modern St Kildans also wish to preserve the islands' wildlife, though these days this is for its intrinsic value rather than its value for exploitation. Those wishing to safeguard St Kilda's marine life must first evaluate the threats to it. St Kilda is relatively far from sources of industrial pollution, and it might be considered a suitable baseline 'clean' site. This may be the case for some 'pollutants'. However, fulmars from St Kilda have among the highest levels of cadmium yet recorded for a living wild animal, in their liver[18] and also have high levels of mercury. These high levels are probably relatively harmless though, for cadmium is bound to a protein which detoxifies it, and mercury is stored in a non-toxic form.[19] Both of these chemicals are regarded as pollutants in some circumstances, but also occur in relatively high concentrations in marine organisms. Fulmars, as predators at the top end of the food chain, are relatively adapted to these chemicals.

St Kilda has several designations, both national and international, to indicate its importance to nature conservation. The designations aim to prevent activities that may damage the wildlife of the islands. Both the designations and the understanding of activities that may cause damage rely on the work of scientists working on the islands. Unfortunately, so far only the land of the St Kilda archipelago has been designated, and is receiving some protection. However, as described above, the land and sea of St Kilda are intimately related. Some activities at sea could seriously damage the wildlife of the islands. Perhaps one of the main challenges to explorers of St Kilda in the future is to devise mechanisms that will shield the wildlife from the threats caused by human activities at sea.

Notes and References

[1] Sands, J 1878, *Out of the world; or, Life in St Kilda*, MacLachlan and Stewart, Edinburgh.

[2] Sands 1878.

[3] Harrisson, T H and Lack, D 1934, 'The breeding birds of St Kilda', *Scottish Naturalist* 1934: 59–69.

[4] Harris, M P and Murray, S 1978 *Birds of St Kilda* Institute of Terrestrial Ecology, Cambridge.

[5] Tasker, M L, Moore, P R and Schofield, R A 1988 'The seabirds of St Kilda, 1987' *Scottish Birds* vol 15: 21–9.

[6] Murray, S and Wanless, S 1986 'The status of the gannet in Scotland 1984–5' *Scottish Birds* vol 14: 74–85.

[7] Harris, M P and Rothery, P, 1988, 'Monitoring of puffin burrows on Dùn, St Kilda, 1977–87' *Bird Study* vol 35: 97–9.

[8] Furness, R W and Todd, C M 1984 'Diets and feeding of fulmars *Fulmarus glacialis* during the breeding season: a comparison between St Kilda and Shetland colonies' *Ibis* vol 126: 379–87.

[9] Furness and Todd 1984.

[10] Furness and Todd 1984.

[11] Harris, M P and Hislop, J R G 1981 'The food of young puffins *Fratercula arctica' Journal of Zoology*, London vol 195: 213–36.

[12] Harris, M P 1984 *The Puffin*, Poyser, Calton.

[13] Taylor, G K 1982 *Predator-prey interactions between great black-backed gulls and puffins and the evolutionary significance of puffin grouping behaviour.* PhD Thesis, University of St Andrews.

[14] Leaper, G M; Webb, A; Benn, S; Prendergast, H D V; Tasker, M L and Schofield, R 1988 'Seabird studies around St Kilda, June 1987' *Nature Conservancy Council Chief Scientist Directorate report no. 804.*

[15] Sutherland, D G 1984 'The submerged landforms of the St Kilda archipelago, Western Scotland' *Marine Geology* vol 58: 435–42.

[16] Howson, C M and Picton, B E 1985 'A sublittoral survey of St Kilda' *Nature Conservancy Council Chief Scientist Directorate report no. 595.*

[17] See for example Cadman, P; Ellis, J; Geiger, D and Piertney, S 1993 'A survey of the marine fauna of the St Kilda archipelago' *Report of Department of Marine Biology*, University of Wales, Swansea.

[18] Bull, K R; Murton, R K; Osborn, D and Ward, P 1977 'High levels of cadmium in Atlantic seabirds and sea-skaters' *Nature* vol 269: 507–9.

[19] Osborn, D 1978 'A naturally occurring cadmium and zinc binding protein from the liver and kidney of *Fulmarus glacialis,* a pelagic North Atlantic seabird' *Biochemical Pharmacology* vol 27: 822–4.

Chapter 5

Soay Sheep

Peter Jewell

More than any other feature of the natural history of the archipelago of St Kilda, the Soay sheep are a treasure of surpassing value. They were neglected by zoologists and rather overlooked by naturalists probably because they were thought of as just another domestic animal. In fact they are a remarkable survival of the type of domestic sheep that people kept in the Bronze Age. Another similar population did survive on the island of Lille Dimon in the Faroes, but they were shot out at the end of the last century leaving the sheep on the island of Soay as the unique example of this ancient and primitive type. Their preservation was made more secure when a section of the population was moved from Soay to Hirta in 1932. (The islanders had kept the ubiquitous Hebridean Blackface on Hirta and Boreray. The Hirta flock was rounded up and sold on the mainland at the evacuation of 1930. The Boreray flock was left to fend for itself and still flourishes there.) The Soays now form a reference point for studies of numerous breeds of sheep, especially the primitive breeds such as Hebridean, Manx Loaghtan and North Ronaldsay, as well as providing material to compare with bones from archaeological sites and with ancient parchments. (Soays which we see elsewhere today are descendants of the St Kilda population, taken off the island to form managed flocks on estates and in zoos.)

In addition, this confined population was seen to provide potential for the intensive study of a 'feral' herbivore. Feral describes a group of animals descended from domestic stock that now lives as a self-sustaining population in the wild; many such feral populations present difficult conservation problems throughout the world.[1] For example, many tropical islands carry populations of sheep or goats put there by seafarers in the past, and these herbivores threaten to obliterate the indigenous plants and animals. In particular, on the island of Aldabra and in the Galapagos Islands feral goats compete for food with the giant tortoises.

Figure 52.   Soays silhouetted on Ruaival with Dùn in the background.

The first serious attempt to assess the numbers of feral sheep on Hirta was made by Dr J Morton Boyd in 1952[2] when he established an effective routine for their census. This was repeated each year from 1955 to 1958 (see Figure 53), and, with modifications, in all subsequent years. Boyd recognised that this extraordinary population of sheep was much too interesting to neglect and so in 1959 he sought the support of two research officers from the Hill Farming Research Organisation, Dr John Doney and Dr Graham Gunn. I had independently developed an interest in the sheep because of their value in archaeology and because of the light they might throw on the nature of early domesticates. It was also possible that their study might provide a start in the better understanding of the ecology of mammalian herbivores elsewhere.[1] The Soay sheep with no competitors and no predators appeared to provide a useful simplified model. Above all it was hoped that their study would provide some direct evidence for the way in which selective forces in evolution may operate, and, as will be seen in what follows, this aspiration has been fulfilled. I helped to form the Soay Research Team in 1960, and as I had just been appointed to the first research fellowship created at the Zoological Society of London I was able to devote my time to field work: I made my first visit to the island in the spring of that year. We were also joined by Dr Cedric Milner, an agricultural botanist from the Nature Conservancy.

Early Investigations

When the newly formed Soay Research Team arrived on Hirta in May 1960 they were confronted by a large number of sheep carcasses scattered throughout the Village. When counts were made it emerged that over half the ewes and three-quarters of the rams that had been seen the previous year were dead. Mortality was particularly heavy amongst the lambs of the previous year (just becoming yearlings) and the oldest age classes.[3] The population had 'crashed' but so many sheep had died that we feared some specific nutritional disease might be involved. We knew, however, of the 'boom and bust' population cycles that characterise other populations of mammals, and the data we had collected up to that time did give a hint that numbers might be cyclic (see Figure 53). It was evident that starvation and stress played an important part in the mortality. It was decided to

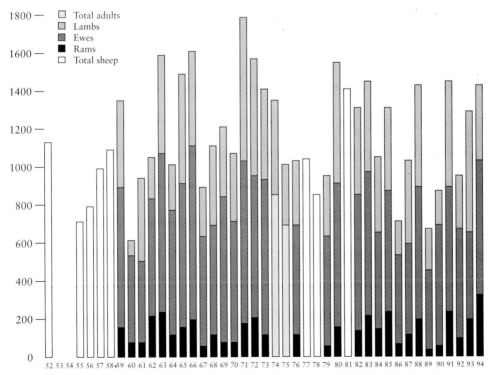

Figure 53. Year to year fluctuations in numbers of Soay sheep on Hirta, St Kilda, taken from the summer census in May or June. In some years a breakdown into the several categories of sheep was not achieved and counts were made by inexperienced volunteers.

Figure 54.   Dark and light-coloured Soays on Ruaival.

initiate a study that would involve regular visits to the island every year.

As Soays are not managed, they cannot be rounded up in the usual way. Methods of catching the sheep for examination had to be found. We tried driving the sheep into nets with little success and resorted to trapping them at night in the cleitean and transferring them to a holding pen in one of the old houses. The lambs could be caught by hand soon after birth and they were weighed, sexed and tagged. Dalton ear-tags were used, of a distinctive colour for each successive year, so that cohorts could be readily recorded in subsequent observations. In addition, a few adult sheep were given collars of distinctive colours. Adult sheep were assigned to age classes on the basis of the eruption sequence of incisor and canine teeth; they were weighed and various body measurements were taken using large callipers specially designed by the Hill Farming Research Organisation.[3]

In the following year the population was well on the way to recovery. Hardly any sheep died in the winter of 1960–1 and the 1961 lamb crop was abundant and early.[4] During the four years 1960 to 1963 much basic information about the biology of the sheep was established. The sheep are dimorphic in many respects: dark brown and light fawn coat colour occur in the ratio 3:1, and amongst ewes rather more than half are polled, the remainder carrying horns. A primitive feature of the Soay is the natural casting of the fleece every spring and the pattern of casting was recorded. Growth rates over the first few years of life were established. It soon became apparent that the sheep, at least the ewes, were firmly attached to the range where they were born, or were 'hefted' to it as hill farmers would say, and individuals remained in a very restricted home range from year to year.[3,5]

When 1963 arrived it was clear that the numbers of sheep had attained a new peak and heavy mortality in 1964 was anticipated. Moreover the researchers had not always been present at lambing time in April and more information was needed on sex ratios at birth, and the weights of lambs. It was decided therefore that a big increase in the research effort should be made in 1964.

Intensifying Research in 1964

In February 1964 three veterinary surgeons, I A Cheyne, W M Foster and J B Spence, established themselves on Hirta with a make-shift veterinary laboratory and post-mortem room in the Village. They stayed until May and during that time witnessed a spectacular die-off of almost half the over-wintering sheep population. The study of this mortality was intensive. Some post-mortem examinations were carried out on the hill but most carcasses were brought back to the post-mortem room. The dead animals were weighed and examined for lesions and external parasites. The contents of the thorax and all of the guts were carefully examined and the numbers of internal parasites assessed: samples of tissue were taken from lung, liver, kidney, heart, bone marrows, thyroid and adrenal glands. Any urine in the bladder was tested for glucose, and the brain and joints were opened and examined. Blood and faecal samples were taken from live animals. All this required a lot of equipment to be taken to St Kilda including a centrifuge, microscope, thermos jars, and a portable colorimeter for iron and haemoglobin estimations. Much clean glassware was needed and a butane bunsen burner provided a hot enough flame to draw the great numbers of glass pipettes required.

The results of all this work provided basic information about the health of the sheep, the parasite burden they endure and the mineral and metabolic stresses to which they might be subject.[6] No specific disease was found to account for mortality, however, and it became evident that lack of available food in late winter, combined with the debilitating effects of parasitic worms in guts and lungs, was the straightforward cause of death.

One further study concerning the health of the sheep must be mentioned, and this involved an examination of the mineral status of the skeleton and the dental condition of the sheep in 1965 and 1966. This was done by D Benzie and J C Gill of the Rowett Research Institute who took a portable X-ray unit to the island and made an extensive series of radiographs of the limbs and teeth of living sheep.[7] A loss of bone density was detected in pregnant ewes but there was a marked improvement by a few weeks after parturition. In general the mineral status of the bones of Soay sheep was found to be good – comparable to that of mainland sheep on good grazing. Development was slower, however, and skeletal maturity was not reached until five years of age which is fully one year later than in mainland hill sheep.

The teeth of the Soays proved to be remarkably sound and superior to that of most mainland breeds. Most Soays retain the incisor and canine teeth till six years of age or more and the teeth remain embedded firmly in the alveolar tissue of the bone. Possibly the mineral status of the pastures of Hirta is high, being enhanced by sea-spray. It may also be supposed that there is strong natural selection for sound and persistent teeth. (We shall see later that new studies throw light on the importance of incisor teeth.)

Two Research Students Live On Hirta

It was obvious that to find out more about the Soay sheep population they must be studied throughout the whole year. More information was needed about the events during the rut in November, the behaviour of the sheep during winter, the exact incidence and pattern of lambing and the diet of the sheep in every season. Two research students were recruited to live on Hirta from 1964 to 1967. Peter Grubb studied population dynamics and David Gwynne studied the botanical composition of the swards and the diet of the sheep.

With the cyclic nature of the population size, and the intermittent incidence of heavy mortality, it soon emerged that each annual cohort of lambs had very different prospects of survival and so made markedly different contributions to the size of the adult population. The numbers of sheep build up over three or four years and then there is a 'crash' when half the population may die. It is a 'boom and bust' economy.

Sheep die at quite specific times in the cycle. Mortality is strongly density-dependent. That is to say the larger the population the greater the proportion of sheep likely to die. Deaths occur in late winter, in March and April, at a time when the bodily reserves of the sheep are at a low ebb and when there is little new growth in the pastures. Moreover, April is the month of lambing so in a crash year many pregnant ewes die and even if they survive and manage to deliver their lambs they are in a poor condition, and produce little milk so the lambs die. Striking examples of such years are 1960, 1964 and 1967, seen in Figure 53. By

Figure 55.   Weighing sheep in the Village.

contrast, a year after a crash, the density of sheep is lower and virtually no sheep die at all. Lambs born in such a spring have a flying start and they are likely to be long-lived and contribute in an important way to further proliferation.

Peter Grubb was able to record many details of the pattern of mortality. Male and female lambs are born in equal numbers and the sexes suffer similar neonatal mortality. There is no difference in the birth weight of male and female lambs (but recent work has shown that as population density rises birth weights fall).[16] Lambs of light birth weight are more likely to die than heavier ones and twins are more likely to die than singletons, perhaps partly because individual twins are also lighter in weight. Moreover the lambs of lightweight ewes, and very young ewes, are more likely to die.

Despite the fact that equal numbers of male and female lambs enter the population every year the ratio of rams to ewes in the adult population is heavily biased in favour of females. Over a series of years the ratio varies from one ram to three ewes to one to eight. As population density rises so the number of lambs that die in their first winter of life rises. More males than females die at this time and in subsequent winters rams continue to die at a constant rate. Ewes, on the

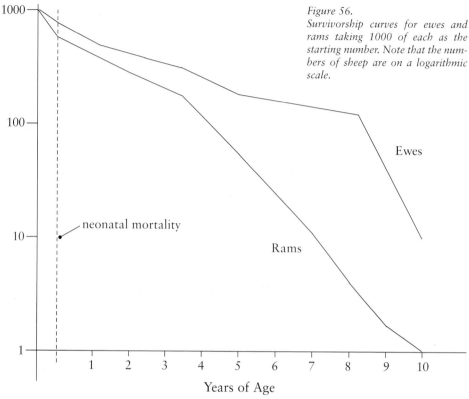

Figure 56.
Survivorship curves for ewes and rams taking 1000 of each as the starting number. Note that the numbers of sheep are on a logarithmic scale.

other hand, show good survival through the middle years of life and exhibit a survival curve that is characteristic of many large mammals (Figure 56).[8] It is a challenge to understand this differential mortality. It was noted that young rams grow faster than ewes and lose more body weight in winter. During the rut in November the rams spend most time in competition with one another and chasing ewes, and little time feeding.

Longevity

A few sheep have long life spans and live through several crashes. The environment is not harsh but it is certainly stressful and the sheep that live through the privation of more than one winter crash must be tough. The longest-lived ewe that was recorded was born in 1967 (she had a pink eartag of that year) and was last seen in 1982 at the age of 15. Another born in 1979 was still alive in 1993 at 14 and one born the year before died in 1993 at 15. Several other ewes have lived to be 13 and 12 years old. For a ram to survive ten years is very rare. A dark ram tagged in 1980 was last seen alive in 1990. Rams have well-marked annual growth zones on their horns and a few skulls have been found with nine such growth rings. Most rams, however, die before they are six years old (see Figure 56).

The Sheep and Their Food Supply

David Gwynne and Cedric Milner set about unravelling the complex interactions between the sheep and their pastures. Samples of vegetation were collected through all seasons. Its botanical composition and mineral content were determined by analysis at the West of Scotland College of Agriculture (Auchencruive, Ayrshire). Samples of faeces were collected regularly and by identifying the plant fragments in them the diet of the sheep was determined. This information was supplemented by knowledge of the movements of the sheep and their grazing intensity on different plant communities.

Of particular interest were the changes in the selection of plants through the year. The growth of grass begins in early April and from then on the standing crop rises to a peak in August. During the months from March to July the digestibility of the herbage also increases greatly. The sheep feed avidly, selecting the young growth of the grass species *Agrostis, Holcus* and *Poa*. As the season advances,

Figure 57. A light ram at the end of winter.

however, the sheep range more widely and by June are taking in a high proportion of heather from the hills. This *Calluna* is a valuable component of the winter diet but in late winter the sheep are eating much dead and dry vegetation and their stomachs contain a lot of moss of low nutritional value. In the months from December to March the intake of digestible protein falls below that needed for maintenance and production, certainly too low for pregnant and lactating ewes. In years of high numbers this situation will be exacerbated by competition between the sheep for food and by the levels of their parasitic burdens. We shall see later how natural selection may be operating through these factors.

The Reproductive Cycle and Timing of Births

The pattern of mating and lambing in the Soay sheep is no different from the well-studied sequence in commercial breeds, but in the latter, of course, it is the farmer

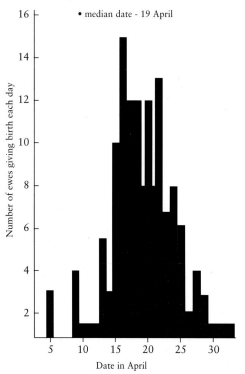

Figure 58a. The number of ewes giving birth day by day during April 1993.

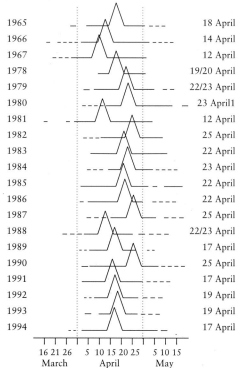

Figure 58b. The observed period of lambing, year by year, together with the dates by which half the lambs had been born (median dates). The dashes indicate the few exceptionally early or late births. Based on detailed records of the type shown in Figure 58a.

82

or the shepherd who decides when to put the rams with the ewes, so determining the time of mating, and the number of rams used is very limited so competition between them is minimal. The population of Soay sheep on Hirta offers a unique opportunity to see how free-ranging sheep, with a large complement of rams, respond to the seasons without any interference by people.

A full record of all lambs born in the Village Bay has now been obtained for 18 years. In most of these years the median date of lambing has been within a few days of 20th April, and births in the whole population of ewes are clumped around this date (Figure 58a). Figure 58b illustrates this striking consistency over the years. This must mean that lambs born at this time have the greatest chance of survival and there is strong selection against ewes that do not conform.[9] Gestation length is 151 days with little variation and the distribution of births accurately mirrors the distribution of conceptions in November. It is known that the timing of oestrus ('heat' or sexual receptivity) in sheep is a direct response to changing daylight length. The Soay sheep have evidently evolved a remarkable physiological sensitivity to the shortening days of the northern autumn.

Figure 59.   *A confrontation between two rams.*

Mating Success

As all the ewes come into oestrus in mid November, each for only one or two days, there is intense competition between the rams to mate with them. Rams do not gather harems of ewes and attempt to defend them (as red deer stags do, for example) but there is open competition between all rams. By threats, butting and contests of stength the rams establish a hierarchy among themselves. The dominant rams successfully defend and 'tend', or consort with, the most ewes.[10] Interestingly enough, the ram lambs, although no match for the older ones, join in this process and this undoubtedly contributes to their loss of condition and likelihood of not surviving the ensuing winter. Perhaps this behaviour is not as ill-adaptive as it may seem, however, because in years following a crash, when the numbers of adult rams can be very low ram lambs greatly outnumber the adults and could achieve precocious reproductive success.[9] (Ram lambs reach sexual maturity and are fertile at six months of age.) The question of which rams actually achieve paternity and become successful sires had to await the application of DNA fingerprinting that has been used from 1988 onwards.

The behavioural and botanical research continued to the early 1970s and the output of over a decade of intensive work culminated in the publication *Island Survivors: the Ecology of the Soay Sheep of St Kilda* in 1974.[8]

Research on Soay Sheep Skeletons

Research effort in the mid 1970s was low key, but one valuable resource was explored and that is the abundant sheep skeletons found in the cleitean and the large scatter of bones that occur on Hirta. Dr Philip Armitage and I collected a large sample of known-age skeletons, and a random sample of bones, and added them to the research collection of mammalian material in The Natural History Museum, London. A particular purpose was to provide a collection of bones of the most primitive domestic sheep – the Soay – for comparison with ancient bones from archaeological sites. Subsequently, in collaboration with Dr Juliet Clutton-Brock, the Curator of Osteology at the Museum, the bones were measured and their anatomical features recorded. They were then used to test the reliability of accepted distinction from the bones of goats. This has provided a corpus of information of great practical use in archaeozoological research.[11] The bones of sheep from many prehistoric sites prove to be similar to Soay bones and so the type of sheep husbanded, their meat yield and perhaps feed type can be reconstructed. The abundant sheep bones excavated from the famous neolithic site of Skara Brae in the Orkneys revealed these sheep to be similar to the Soays, but with somewhat longer legs.

Investigating Factors Affecting Male Survival by the Creation of Wethers

Towards the end of the 1970s I initiated a new approach to the question of differential mortality between males and females. To try and reveal some of the factors involved it was decided to castrate a small cohort of male lambs so removing their reproductive drive. It is well known that castrates, or wethers as they are called, do not attempt to mate ewes in the breeding season, although they can be readily induced to do so by the injection of the male hormone, testosterone. Wethers can comprise an interesting class in a population. On the island of North Ronaldsay, for example, about a third of the seaweed-eating sheep on the beaches are wethers, where, by competing for resources but failing to breed, they must help to buffer fluctuations in population number. In April 1978 I visited Hirta with a veterinary colleague, Professor Colin Finn, and 14 male lambs were castrated. Eight more were castrated the following year. No problems having arisen in these pilot studies a definitive cohort of 50 castrates was created in 1980. Similar numbers of entire males, born and tagged at the

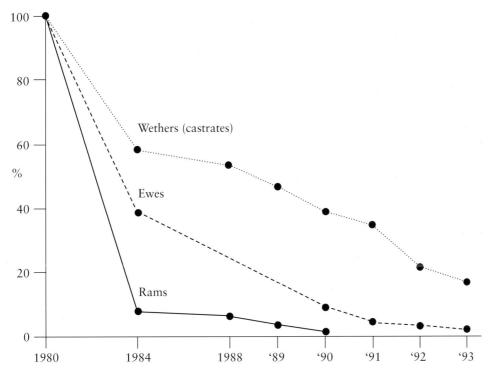

Figure 60.   The survival of wethers (castrates) compared with that of entire rams and ewes standardised as a percentage of the starting numbers.

same time, were marked as controls. In this way 72 wethers with 68 entire male controls (a few having died in the first few weeks of life) entered the population. Their subsequent fate, together with that of tagged female lambs from the same years is shown in Figure 60. It soon became clear that the wethers would outlive the rams:[12] the ability of the wethers to survive is remarkable; 20 were still alive when all the control rams were dead and 11 are still alive today (July 1994) being from 16 to 14 years old. Their survival is better than that of females as Figure 60 shows. The castrates have been observed to avoid the mêlée of the rut and to spend much more time feeding through November than do rams and ram lambs. The condition of wethers, by visual scoring in early summer, is better than either rams or ewes. It is concluded that for rams the diversions of the rut and the reduced time spent feeding are a key factor in their poor survival rate.

1985: A New Phase of Research Starts

By 1985 the Soay sheep study had been running for 25 years. Meantime another study of a grazing mammal on an Hebridean island had been in progress for 15 years – the study of red deer on the island of Rum by Dr Tim Clutton-Brock.[13] He had formed a number of hypotheses about survival, fitness and individual reproductive success in this population and he wanted to test these on a population of another species. The Hirta population of Soay sheep presented ideal opportunities for comparison and for contrast – for example the sheep have a shorter life cycle, mature more rapidly and show persistent instability of population size compared with red deer. In addition ewes often have twins of one sex or mixed sexes, whereas red deer hinds hardly ever have twins. This gives many permutations for the study of mother-offspring relationships. Dr Clutton-Brock accepted our offer of the well-documented Village Bay population of Soay sheep for further study and supported by Dr Steve Albon and other colleagues a new phase of research began in 1985, carried out by the Large Animal Research Group (LARG) of the Department of Zoology at Cambridge University.

A bigger research effort, involving a larger number of people than the former Soay Research Team could muster, was soon under way. Sheep were captured with immobilizing darts as well as by hand and it was not long before the entire Village population had been caught and tagged. Sheep carrying small ear tags were retagged with large ones whose numbers could be more easily read from a distance. Growth rates were needed and this called for repeated capture of individuals, so summer catch-ups to weigh as many sheep as possible, and also take blood samples from them, were organised – no easy task, but this was where Dr Oliver Dansie and his deer-catching team came to the rescue. His team (now the Mammal Conservation Trust to whom we are greatly indebted for support) own huge lengths of netting that they use to help the owners of deer parks to manage their herds. In August 1989 we established a routine for Hirta. The nets were quickly erected to surround the sheep grazing in the Village meadows and then the sheep, with no escape, could be gently driven into a holding pen.

Considerable financial support was forthcoming from government Research Councils and other sources so that research assistants could again be placed on Hirta for extensive periods of time and extra helpers could be assembled at critical periods. Regular censuses of the study area enabled us to follow individuals from birth to death and from 1985 to the present over 95% of the lambs born in Village Bay were caught and tagged each year. Those not tagged at birth (and so not of precisely known age) but caught later as adults, had their ages estimated from incisor eruption or, after death, by counting growth layers in the cemention of the teeth. (This specialised technique was carried out for us by Rolf Langvatn at the Norwegian Institute for Nature Research, Trondheim, Norway.) All information is instantly recoverable from a computer database.

A 'Key Factor' Analysis

The first question to be resolved was the relative importance of the factors that contribute to mortality.[14] Several factors can be identified – summer mortality, winter mortality, animals disappearing without trace, and also, perhaps not so obviously, ewes failing to breed at all (being barren that year) or having only one lamb when they have the potential to have twins (low fecundity). To find which was the key factor an analytical technique known as Key Factor Analysis was applied. In this technique the proportion of the total losses due to each factor is calculated and standardised over several years so that the factor making the biggest contribution is identified. With this factor accounted for, the next most important factor can be identified, and so on. The results were unequivocal: the number lost from the population during the winter was the key factor. By far the greater proportion of this number were sheep whose deaths could be confirmed because their carcasses were found. Rams were more strongly, and adversely, affected by rising population density than females. Interestingly the proportion of adult ewes lambing was not affected by rising population density though the proportion bearing twins tended to decline. On the other hand many fewer young ewes (conceiving at seven months of age) bore lambs when population density was high.[14] During the course of this research the standing crop of live grasses and herbs was measured by clipping and weighing the dried vegetation from sample plots. The weights confirmed that the available food declined as population size increased.

Persistent Instability of the Hirta Population

The changing responses of the Soay sheep, described above, are similar to the responses of the red deer population on Rum but in one important respect the sheep are different. The red deer (and other animal populations) show a linear relationship (plotted on a logarithmic scale) between winter mortality and population size but, in the sheep, mortality is slight at low and intermediate densities and then rises rapidly and drastically at high densities. In this persistent instability the sheep exhibit an unusual exponential relationship. The causes of this are still under investigation[15,16] but the fact that the Soay sheep are a feral population of a *domestic* animal must be kept in mind. Natural buffers against the ill-effects of rising population density, such as reduced fecundity and delayed puberty, may have been reduced by selection under domestication.

In contrast to other ungulates, including the red deer, it has been found that the Soay sheep show no sex differences in growth rates and in sucking behaviour in the first six weeks of life.[16] This is surprising and is under further investigation; again it may stem from changes under domestication.

Parasite Burdens

A new investigation of the parasitic worms that infest the Soay sheep has been undertaken by Frances Gulland, another of the many research students who have written their PhD theses about the sheep.[17,18]

Previous investigations in the 1960s had shown that the Soay sheep carry heavy infestations of parasitic worms in the gut. This was presumed to be a contributory cause of death but its relative importance was not known. Between 1988 and 1990, a period that spanned a population crash, the parasite burden on Hirta was closely followed. The levels of infective larvae on the pastures were measured and counts were made of parasite eggs in the faeces of sheep of all ages and both sexes. The prevalence of parasites was higher in rams than ewes throughout the study. A dramatic peak in egg counts from all sheep occurred in March and April 1989 and this was the time when the sheep were in poorest condition in a year of population crash (see Figure 53). There was an accompanying increase in infestation by lung worms.

At the same time that the parasite cycle in the Village population of sheep was being followed, a telling experiment was carried out to test the effect of giving an anthelminthic drug. In August 1988, 52 sheep were dosed with boluses that release albendazole into the rumen over a period of a hundred days. This treatment did not prevent sheep from dying but the survival time of treated ewes and young rams was considerably better than that of untreated controls. Moreover, in a similar experiment carried out in 1991–2[19] female lambs and yearling males given albendazole boluses survived significantly better than untreated controls. In a complementary experiment on a small group of captive Soay sheep kept at the field station of the Royal Veterinary College (North Mimms, Hertfordshire) it was found that with good feeding none died despite having a similar parasite burden to the sheep on Hirta. The earlier conclusion[8] that deaths during a crash are caused by starvation exacerbated by parasite infestations is clearly substantiated.

The Role of Parasites in Natural Selection

The conclusive demonstration that parasites play a key role in the survival of the Soay sheep is a satisfactory outcome of a great deal of painstaking research, but a result of much greater significance has emerged from an associative investigation of an accompanying genetic polymorphism in the sheep.[19] Dr Josephine Pemberton, of the Institute of Cell, Animal and Population Biology at Edinburgh University, has played an active role in the recent investigations and she has analysed the occurrence of certain genetic markers, using the blood samples taken from the large numbers of sheep caught each summer. (Indeed, Dr Pemberton is a

Figure 61.   The author putting an ear tag on a lamb.

member of the original deer-catching team who have so greatly facilitated research by bringing their nets to St Kilda.) The particular genetic marker investigated is called Adenosine deaminase (Ada for short). It is an enzyme and two alternative genes (alleles) occur that produce a 'fast' (F) and 'slow' (S) type of molecule. Each sheep has two alleles for each gene and so may belong to one of three genotypes: homozygous (FF and SS) or heterozygous (FS). A total of 1101 live Soay sheep have been typed at Ada since 1985. To simplify the story, what has been discovered is as follows.

Over three successive crashes mortality was significantly different between individuals of the three different genotypes: FF animals were most likely to die and FS animals most likely to survive, whilst SS animals were intermediate. The burden of parasitic worms was found to differ between the three genotypes in a way consistent with these patterns of mortality. In August heterozygous (FS) females are less likely to have worm eggs in their faeces than homozygous (FF and SS) females. At lambing the rise in faecal egg count that always occurs at this time was highest in FF females. In autumn, during the November rut, when males feed little, lose body weight and get into poor condition, the heterozygous rams (FS) had, on average, lower faecal egg counts than homozygous rams (FF and SS). The observed balance at the Ada locus offers a clear example of heterozygous advantage and has interesting parallels with certain human conditions. The best known of these is sickle cell anaemia where people in malarious areas in West Africa survive the disease if they are heterozygous for this gene.

In general, direct evidence for the maintenance of genetic variation by parasite-associated selection is scarce, but it is an important idea in theories of evolutionary fitness and these results are a rewarding outcome of the present intensive research.

New Work On Male Reproductive Success

A further test of whether mating activity is a cause of poor male survival has been carried out by Ian Stevenson, a research student with LARG. In August 1991 he gave a group of ram lambs a single injection of the progestagen Depro-Provera. This synthetic substance is similar to one of the female sex-hormones; in males it inhibits the formation of the male sex-hormone, testosterone, and so blocks sexual and aggressive behaviour. Behavioural watches, conducted during the subsequent rut, confirmed that the treated males neither took part in mating activity nor reduced their feeding rate. Twice as many ram lambs in this group survived in the following winter (a crash) compared with ram lambs in a control group that had no treatment. This result substantiates the spectacular results already demonstrated by castration that has led to a long-term increase in survival.

The application of DNA profiling (a development of genetic fingerprinting in use since 1985 for establishing parenthood in people) to quantify reproductive success has now been initiated by David Bancroft, a research student of Dr Pemberton. Previously, the only measure of the success of individual rams was a behavioural one. The number of ewes with which rams consorted during the ewes' oestrus was thought to indicate their likely success as sires. The new evidence shows that this is not necessarily so and rams that had not been seen mating gained significant paternity. Of particular interest was the revelation that many ram lambs were successful sires. This was pronounced in the mating season after a crash when surviving adult rams were few and ram lambs relatively numerous. This result could explain the precocious behaviour of ram lambs already referred to on page 84.

New Work On Jaw Morphology

Current new work of a different kind is being carried out by Dr Andrew Illius of the Institute of Cell, Animal and Population Biology, University of Edinburgh and Dr Iain Gordon of the Macaulay Land Use Research Institute, Aberdeen. They have recognised the importance of the food-gathering power of the incisor teeth whose robustness had been demonstrated by earlier X-ray work. In the new work the breadth of the incisor arcade was measured in all the sheep captured during the summer of 1991. In the following winter there was a crash but it was found that the survivors were the individuals with significantly broader incisor plus canine teeth. This provides direct evidence of natural selection acting on incisor arcade structure. This conclusion is supported by the observation that young Soay sheep show earlier maturation of incisor breadth than other grazing ruminants, and it appears that this may have arisen as a result of density-dependent selection.

Aspirations Fulfilled

When the Nature Conservancy (as it was then) first established nature reserves it was a declared intention that, in addition to protecting and preserving interesting and important habitats, these places should become 'open-air laboratories'. It was in this spirit that our work on the Soay sheep was initiated. It began in 1959, only one year after the Nature Conservancy took over the management of St Kilda as a National Nature Reserve. I believe that the subsequent endeavours in research, particularly the continuous investigation of the Soay sheep, have admirably demonstrated the value of this policy of creating open-air laboratories. In this way long-term observations and experiments have been given the security they need. Most recently the expansion of the research into the incisive analysis of population dynamics has demonstrated the importance of uninterrupted observations and experiment. Dr Tim Clutton-Brock has shown how these results can be enhanced by comparisons with other long-running studies. Dr Steve Albon, who has contributed much to the recent work, has now moved from LARG to join the research institute of the Zoological Society in London. The Society, therefore, is again taking an active interest in the continuing study of the Soay sheep that I initiated for them over 35 years ago. These long-term studies can probe more deeply into the processes of evolution itself and add profoundly to our better understanding of the world we live in.

Notes and References

[1] Jewell, P A 1961 'The wild sheep of St Kilda' *New Scientist* vol 114, 268–71.

[2] Boyd, J M 1956 'The sheep population of Hirta, St Kilda, 1955' *Scot. Nat.* vol 68, 10–13.

[3] Boyd, J M; Doney, J M; Gunn, R G and Jewell, P A 1964 'The Soay sheep of the island of Hirta, St Kilda. A study of a feral population' *Proc. Zool. Soc. Lond.* vol 142, 129–63.

[4] Jewell, P A 1966 'Breeding season and recruitment in some British mammals confined on small islands' *Symp. Zool. Soc. Lond.* vol 15, 89–111.

[5] Jewell, P A 1966 'The concept of home range in mammals' *Symp. Zool. Soc. Lond.* vol 18, 85–109.

[6] Cheyne, I A; Foster, W M and Spence, J B 1974 'The incidence of disease and parasites in the Soay sheep population of Hirta' Chapter 13 in ref. 8.

[7] Benzie, D and Gill, J C 1974 'Radiography of the skeletal and dental condition of the Soay sheep' Chapter 12 in ref. 8.

[8] Jewell, P A; Milner, C and Morton Boyd, J 1974 *Island survivors: the ecology of the Soay sheep of St Kilda*, Athlone Press: London.

[9] Jewell, P A 1989 'Factors that affect fertility in a feral population of sheep' *Zool. J. Linnean Soc.* vol 95, 163–74.

[10] Grubb, P 1974 'The rut and behaviour of Soay rams' Chapter 8 in ref. 8.

[11] Clutton-Brock, J; Dennis-Byran, K; Armitage, P J and Jewell, P A 1990 'Osteology of the Soay sheep' *Bull. Br. Mus. Nat. Hist. (Zool)*, vol 56(1), 1–56.

[12] Jewell, P A 1986 'Survival in a feral population of primitive sheep on St Kilda, Outer Hebrides, Scotland' *National Geog. Research* vol 2, 401–6 .

[13] Clutton-Brock, T H; Guinness, F E and Albon, S D 1982 *Red deer: behaviour and ecology of two sexes*, Edinburgh Univ. Press: Edinburgh.

[14] Clutton-Brock, T H; Price, O F; Albon, S D and Jewell, P A, 1991 'Persistent

instability and population regulation in Soay Sheep' *J. Anim. Ecol.* vol 60, 593–608.

[15] Clutton-Brock, T H; Price, O F; Albon, S D and Jewell, P A 1992 'Early development and population fluctuations in Soay sheep' *J. Anim. Ecol.* vol 61, 381–96.

[16] Robertson, A; Hiraiwa-Hasegawa, M; Albon, S D and Clutton-Brock, T H 1992 'Early growth and sucking behaviour of Soay sheep in a fluctuating population' *J. Zool. Lond.* vol 227, 661–71.

[17] Gulland, F M D and Fox, M 1992 'Epidemiology of nematode infections of Soay sheep (*Ovis aries L.*) on St Kilda' *Parasitology,* vol 105, 481–92.

[18] Gulland, F M D 1992 'The role of nematode parasites in Soay sheep (*Ovis aries L.*) mortality during a population crash' *Parasitology,* vol 105 493–503.

[19] Gulland, F M D; Albon, S D; Pemberton, J M; Moorcroft, P R and Clutton-Brock, T H 1993 'Parasite-associated polymorphism in a cyclic ungulate population' *Proc. Roy. Soc. B.* vol 254, 7–13.

Chapter 6

St Kilda – Exploring the Future

John Smyth

The islands of St Kilda, jutting upwards through the Atlantic near the edge of the continental shelf, surrounded by clouds and wind and stormy seas, should be one of the least vulnerable parts of Europe, a place where protection and preservation are issues hardly worth considering. Yet they are clearly not inaccessible: hardy representatives of the European land flora and fauna reached them long ago. Humankind and its livestock have come and gone, and come again. Now growing pressures of human population, activity and technology are changing the world round about as never before. How will St Kilda be in the future?

When the Kearton brothers described and photographed the islands a hundred years ago no one could have forecast the changes that were to take place in the following century.[1] No more can we say what the next hundred years will bring. We can only do for the future what seems right to us at this time. For that we need as much information as possible about what we are trying to care for, hence the research reported in previous chapters. We need to assess what threats may come. We need to maintain a climate of public support for what we aim to do. And we can be quite clear that at the end of the 20th century St Kilda is no longer remote, and even if it were that would be no protection.

What comes to St Kilda must come by air or sea. It is no surprise that the islands have great and world-famous seabird colonies. However, the air masses circulating round the northern hemisphere have always been able to carry other things besides birds: the dust from distant volcanic eruptions for example, and now the products of industrial activity and of man-made disasters such as Chernobyl. Natural or human in origin, they are part of the environment of the modern North Atlantic, and rain may bring them back to earth.

The sea has always supplied St Kilda with most of what its life depends on.

Some 40 miles to the west the continental shelf comes to an end and the sea bed slopes downwards into the deep waters of the Rockall Trough. Here a major ocean current moves northwards along the continental slope and its water spreads over the shelf.[2] Its movement is complicated by tidal currents and by wind speed and direction, and it varies also with the season, but overall it moves water northeastwards at something over 2½ kilometres a day.

To the east, over the shelf, it meets with the coastal current. This is water which emerges from the Irish Sea and flows northwards along the Scottish coast, part of it streaming out to the west of the Outer Hebrides. This coastal water is a little less salty from receiving freshwater inflows and, especially in summer, spreads over the top of the saltier, denser Atlantic water.

In spring the upper layer of water over the shelf warms up more quickly than the deeper water and the two layers become effectively separated. Each develops its own circulation and they remain separate and stratified until the autumn or early winter when gales disturb the water so much that the layers overturn and the water column becomes mixed again. This has important consequences for the life of the sea.

The marine economy is largely based on the productive activity of the tiny, single-celled plants which make up the bulk of the plankton, the floating life of the sea. Like other plants they need the energy of sunlight to live and grow, so they are only active in the upper layer of the sea into which light can penetrate. But, like other plants, they also need nutrients – nitrates, phosphates, silicates and others in lesser quantity – which they take in from the water. Most of these substances enter the water from the breakdown of past generations of plankton and other dead organisms which have sunk down to the sea bed to decay. When the sea becomes stratified, therefore, the plants (phytoplankton) in the sunlit upper layers become cut off from their nutrient supplies. When nutrients already in the upper water are exhausted they cannot be replenished until the autumn, so plant production declines sharply just at the time when light and temperature are most favourable for growth.

Around St Kilda, however, the picture is different. The great rocks standing out of the sea bed in the path of the water current have been compared to a teaspoon in a cup of tea, except that in this case the spoon remains still and the water provides the movement.[3] The result is the same: it is stirred, breaking the stratification. Nutrient-rich deeper water is brought to the surface like sugar in the teacup so that phytoplankton in the upper waters is supplied with nutrients and can continue to flourish throughout the summer.

This of course benefits not only the phytoplankton but the small animals which graze it and the larger animals which in turn feed on them. Beneath them the sea bed is also further enriched by additional organic remains sinking down to be recycled, at the same time improving the resources for the community of life at or near the bottom. Thus St Kilda provides its seabirds not only with nest sites but with the other essential for breeding success – a productive zone around it in the sea offering convenient, rich fishing grounds all summer. This also helps to support the varied sea life among the submerged rocks and caves. In the past it created a rich enough resource to sustain a human population over many centuries, in spite of the harsh conditions, and explains the presence still of continental fishing boats to which Mark Tasker has already referred.

Like the wind, however, the water does not only bring benefits. A convenient way for scientists to recognise water coming from the coastal current has been the presence in it of tiny quantities of radioactive caesium, discharged from the Sellafield site of British Nuclear Fuels plc, which includes the Windscale nuclear fuel reprocessing plant.[4] Labelled in this way water from the Irish Sea can be traced right out beyond the Hebrides. This has been used to work out not only the path of the coastal current but the amount of water it carries, the rate of flow and variations between different years. While it may benefit the progress of scientific knowledge this carries a warning for the environment of St Kilda, even although the hydrography of the surrounding seas protects these islands better than most of the Scottish coast.

In this case the quantity of radiocaesium is very small and there is no evidence that it damages anything. It is not, of course, the only radioactive material which now finds its way into the sea. When substances of this sort reach there they may enter the cells of plankton and thus get into the food chain. They pass up it stage by stage (and marine food chains are often very long), becoming more concentrated each time until they reach top predators which accumulate the materials collected by many active organisms below them in the chain. Mark Tasker has already pointed this out in the context of cadmium and mercury in the tissues of seabirds (page 71). Some years ago an observer on St Kilda noticed that ground levels of radioactivity, admittedly very low, increased as one approached areas where the droppings of nesting birds became numerous. The observation was never followed up but it is a reminder that the fate of substances discharged into the sea is not known until they have been traced through all the many pathways which they can follow. We should also remind ourselves that we too are top marine predators, as consumers of sea fish and shellfish.

In these circumstances a fairly close check is kept on radioactive substances in the sea. We now produce, however, and ultimately try to dispose of, a great variety of potentially damaging or actively toxic chemicals by means which are not always known or monitored. Heavy metals, already noted, are among these, as are biocides such as PCBs left over from industrial processes and already known for their damage to marine life. There will be others that are less known now and where they may turn up is beyond accurate prediction.

Many of the discarded products of our current lifestyle are destructible organic materials that have been biodegraded before they reach the open waters around St Kilda. But some are not: walk along the drift line of almost any seashore and see how much of it consists of plastic, multinational in origin and often thrown overboard from ships at sea. Much of this is just wasteful and unsightly, but some of it is lethal – monofilament nylon fishing line and pieces of net, for example. Floating around at the surface of the sea these probably pose a greater threat to seabirds at present than do the chemical discharges. When birds become entangled in them they usually drown. Another threat can be the little white balls into which expanded polystyrene disintegrates. These are ingested by some birds, along with mud and food animals, until they can no longer eat.

Pollution at sea, for most people, conjures up a picture of oil. Unlike many pollutants oil is something which occurs naturally in the sea, in places where oil-bearing rocks are exposed in the sea bed allowing it to leak out naturally. Micro-

Figure 62.   Dead gannet on Stac Lee with fishing line wound round its wing.

organisms capable of degrading oil also occur naturally, using it as a source for their own metabolism. They work slowly, however, on relatively small quantities of oil: the problem that we have created is a result of releasing huge quantities quickly.

As a pollutant oil is obviously nasty – black, smelly and adhesive. A major oil spill is a very visible event, attracting press and television coverage so everyone hears about it. Its effects are quickly illustrated by pathetic pictures of oiled birds and the efforts made to rescue them. If it comes inshore it may cover beaches, threatening the tourist trade, foul coastal equipment and make thousands of pounds-worth of caged salmon unsaleable. Since it is obviously near the top of most conservationists' hate lists, what must we think as the off-shore oil industry edges round the north of Scotland, and tankers meanwhile are urged to avoid the vulnerable waters of the Minch and sail to the west of the Hebrides? What is the danger to St Kilda?

When oil is discharged into or onto the sea it spreads widely over the surface in a slick which moves mainly according to the strength and direction of the wind. The more toxic light fractions are volatile and will mostly escape into the air or dissolve in the water within a few days. In the water they seem to do no more than local damage, although large quantities in the air can cause problems (as they did in Shetland in 1993 following the Braer disaster which involved a relatively light oil).

In high winds some oil may be blown off the surface of the slick as droplets and carried quite long distances. What remains becomes more viscous and water movements mix it into an oil-water emulsion known as mousse, which continues to float for some time. Gradually wind and sea break up the slick and the stormier the conditions the quicker it happens. The Braer oil spill demonstrated not only the hazards of stormy waters for transporting oil but also their benefits in breaking up the slick. Eventually what is left are hard tar-balls.

The main victims of an oil slick are animals which break the surface of the sea – seabirds and marine mammals – so there is particular concern when an oil spill happens near an area where there are concentrations of feeding birds. Oiled feathers rapidly lead to hypothermia and preening results in swallowing oil with possibly toxic effects. Animals which remain beneath the surface seem relatively little affected, although there are questions as to what happens when oil sinks to the sea bed. When it reaches the coast many plants and animals seem to be remarkably resilient, but on an exposed rocky coast – like St Kilda – the oil is kept moving about and dispersal is relatively rapid.

Methods for dealing with an oil slick have become familiar from press accounts. In open water treatment with dispersants may be the only practicable method but the resulting mixture can be more toxic. Skimmers, absorbent devices, floating booms and materials for sinking oil have their uses but in quieter inshore waters. The choice of treatment clearly varies with the place and the conditions, and with the speed of response. Each incident requires careful, skilled assessment and major spillages still strain resources severely. It may be that St Kilda will have to depend greatly on the forces of nature for its protection, if there is oil nearby.

The answer, of course, is to prevent oil spills from happening. If the off-shore industry is to move further west into more exposed and dangerous waters it is to be hoped that technology and practice will also have advanced sufficiently to cope with the conditions. Standards of design and rigorous maintenance of equipment and installations, constant observance of safety procedures, exclusion zones protected by radar surveillance, improved construction and regular inspection of tankers have all been called for, but will still fail if not managed by well trained, high quality staff. This all incurs costs which are inevitably passed on to the users of the product, ourselves. How much extra are we, the public, prepared to pay for petrol and oil products (let alone the knock-on effects on other services) to ensure high standards? If we do not play our part effectively the temptation to cut costs by savings on standards of management and staffing will continue.

Oil, spectacular as an oil disaster may be, may not be so serious a threat to St Kilda as our own lack of knowledge. At least there are natural processes in place which will eventually deal with most of the effects of oil. But in our rapidly changing world we cannot even guess what other threats may arise over the coming decades. St Kilda is inescapably part of a much larger system dominated by the behaviour of humankind. If it is at present relatively untouched that is only because the enclosing human-environment system has chosen to leave it so. That system is now experiencing rates of demographic and technological change that seem to be beyond even human capacities for accurate prediction, adaptation and proper control. How humankind will behave in the future, or will be able to behave, is difficult to foresee.

The bird populations may continue to thrive so long as new environmental threats do not afflict them. The Soay sheep, although not original natives, appear in Peter Jewell's account to have achieved a relationship with their environment which should survive if not severely challenged. For many centuries it seems the same was true of humankind. The native St Kildans must have built up a system of behaviour, attitudes and values that enabled them to survive the vicissitudes of a particularly harsh environment. But in their case things changed: the growth of communication with the outside world brought to the islanders the attitudes and values of more affluent communities which gradually weakened their traditional structure until eventually they could only leave to be absorbed into the wider, and widely different world beyond.

All the people that come to St Kilda now come from that wider community, with their own special reasons for doing so – military, scientific, recreational. How they behave is in conformity with the habits and beliefs of their particular groups within the wider community. At present these favour conservation. The islands are valued as a natural laboratory, the last outcrop of the north west edge of Europe, inaccessible and intractable. They are a simplified system, relatively untouched by human misuse. Backed by a considerable store of accumulated knowledge they offer a prospect of continuing, valuable, long-term research on seabird colonies and grazing mammals, on the history of human habitation, and also possibilities for studies on other aspects of life both above and beneath the sea. Because they are unspoilt they also offer the prospect of acting as an early warning system, to alert people to developing changes that might be more difficult to detect elsewhere, in more complex, more altered environments.

This is how it is now and the combined influence of The National Trust for Scotland, Scottish Natural Heritage and the army have managed to keep it so.

Figure 63.   Early morning. Landing craft leaving St Kilda after unloading on the storm beach.

The first two of these, at least, show every sign of continuing to do so and one can see nothing in the future that might alter their commitment. But might a time eventually come when priorities change or finances fail? In spite of heavy practical constraints on landing there are other interested parties around, now represented only by occasional generally well-behaved visitors, such as enterprising yachtsmen on holiday and continental fishermen in need of shelter. How might their influence change?

Meg Buchanan has mentioned in her introduction the hazard to the islands of rats landing off a visiting boat; one which has so far been avoided. Rats, cats, mink and rabbits are all animals which have wreaked havoc on other islands and could do so here. With less surveillance the first two could easily become established and unfortunately it is possible to imagine scenarios which could bring the other two as well. Commercial developments would not be impossible and who can say how defence strategies might change? On the other hand it is possible that a weakened civilization on the mainland, beset by political and economic problems, might simply shrink away from St Kilda and leave it again to its own devices.

This is idle dreaming. We cannot keep any cherished site, whether an island, a mountain, a woodland or a castle, in total isolation from its surroundings. Inevitably it is influenced by a less protected environment. How well we succeed in caring for our treasures will depend on how highly we regard and care for the rest of the world of which they are part. This in turn may require us to reassess the criteria by which we define our own quality of life both as national and international citizens.

St Kilda is a World Heritage Site, valued for special qualities, a part of our environment which sustains not our bodies but our spirit. We need it to be there even if we cannot reach it. Can we, in these times of rapid change, make the material provisions that are needed to keep it so? Clean sea cannot be created as a barrier round a cherished site any more than clean air. Both are bound to the land and the people who manage it. The health of St Kilda and our own health are all one.

Notes and References

[1] Kearton, R 1897 *With Nature and a Camera*. Cassell & Co Ltd, London.
[2] Ellett, D J 1994 'The oceanographic setting of the Scottish islands'. In Baxter, J M and Usher, M D (eds.): *The Islands of Scotland, a Living Marine Heritage*. HMSO, Edinburgh, 30–53.

[3] Simpson, J H and Tett, P B 1986 'Island stirring effects on phytoplankton growth'. In Bowman, J; Yentsch, M and Peterson, W T (eds.): *Lecture Notes on Coastal and Estuarine Studies, Vol. 17: Tidal Mixing and Plankton Dynamics*, Springer-Verlag, Berlin and Heidelberg, 41–76.

[4] McKay, W A; Baxter, M S; Ellett, D J and Meldrum, D T 1986 'Radiocaesium and circulation patterns west of Scotland'. *Journal of Environmental Radioactivity*, vol 4, 205–32.

Glossary

Actinolite schist	A metamorphic rock. This variety of the rock, schist, includes green-coloured crystals of actinolite amongst its constituent minerals.
Alveolar tissue	Tissue in the sockets of the jaws that bear the teeth.
Anthelminthic drug	A drug used against intestinal worms.
Ard	Early form of plough with a stilt and share, but without coulter or mould-board.
Auger	Instrument for boring in soil or strata, with stem that can be lengthened.
Beehive house	Circular-plan house with overlapping wall courses narrowing to the roof to give a beehive shape.
Belted plaid	Length of cloth – often tartan – arranged to form a 'kilt' and to cover the upper body.
Biocide	A pesticide. Substance that destroys life.
Black house	A dry-stone walled Hebridean house with thatched roof.
Bolus	Large pill.
Bothy	Temporary dwelling.
Byre	Farm unit where cattle are kept.
C14 date	Radiocarbon date based on the deterioration of radioactive isotope of Carbon 14 after death of living matter. This can be measured to provide the date.
Cadmium	A bluish-white metal, in its physical qualities resembling tin, found in small quantities chiefly in zinc ores.

Catechist	One who gives oral instruction in the elements of Christianity, according to a catechism, or by question and answer, but is not an ordained minister.
Centrifuge	A machine rotating at very high speeds, designed to separate solids from liquids, or liquids from other liquids.
Cist	A stone coffin formed of slabs placed on edge and covered on top by a horizontal slab.
Cleit(ean)	Gaelic name for small drystone buildings used for storage.
Colorimeter	Instrument measuring intensity of colour.
Consumption dyke	A wall built from the stones removed from surrounding agricultural land.
Continental shelf	The gently sloping off-shore zone, extending usually to about 200 metres depth.
Continental slope	The steeply sloping sea bed which plunges from the edge of the continental shelf to the deep sea bed.
DNA mapping	Mapping the hereditary information carried by a DNA (de(s)oxyribonucleic acid) molecule.
Dimorphic	Exhibiting two distinct forms.
The Disruption	Move from the established church by a group of Evangelicals in 1843 which resulted in formation of the Free Church of Scotland.
Distaff	Cleft stick, about one metre long, on which wool or flax is wound for spinning by hand.
Dyked forecourt	Drystone-walled enclosed space in front of a building.
EDM (Electronic distance measurement)	An indirect method of measurement incorporating the reflection of a beam of infra-red light from a prism which is placed over the target.
Ecofact	A piece of environmental evidence.
Electrical resistivity survey	Application of a voltage to the ground via metal electrodes inserted into it and measuring its resistance to the flow of electric current. Buried archaeological features, with a different water content, can be identified.

Enzyme	An organic catalyst formed by living cells but not depending on their presence for its action.
Eruption sequence	Sequence in which teeth break through the skin of the gums.
Ethnologist	Person who studies the material culture of societies.
Euphausid	A shrimp-like animal such as krill, living in middle depths and surface waters of sea.
Eviscerated	Disembowelled, or emptied of its vital contents.
Exponential relationship	Relationship in which the logarithm of a number increases linearly with time.
Factor	The manager of a property, not necessarily resident.
Feral	Wild, having reverted from a domesticated state.
Fluvio-glacial features	Features produced by the action of streams which have their source in glacial ice, or the combined action of rivers and glaciers.
Food chain	Succession of organisms connected by feeding relationships, e.g. plant – herbivore – carnivore.
Fractions	Small amount.
Gabbro	A basic igneous rock of crystalline texture.
Genetic polymorphism	The occurrence of different structural forms at different stages in the life-cycle of an individual.
Geo	An inlet of the sea with steep, rocky sides.
Geochemical analysis	Analysis of the chemical composition of the earth's crust.
Geophysical survey	Use of a variety of non-destructive techniques to locate archaeological features. These include magnetic survey and electrical resistivity survey.
Gestation	Period in womb, between conception and birth.
Granophyre	An igneous rock of medium grain size, in which quartz and feldspar are intergrown.
Haemoglobin	Oxygen-carrying pigment contained in the red blood-cells of animals.
Head dyke	A wall marking the perimeter of the cultivated area around a settlement.
Herbivore	An animal which feeds on herbage or plants.

105

Hydrography	Scientific description of the waters of the earth.
Hypogea	Underground dwellings.
Incisor arcade	Bar of bone holding the front, sharp-edged teeth which are adapted for cutting.
Infant tetanus	A form of lockjaw, producing violent spasms.
Lazy bed	A cultivation ridge made with the spade. Often used for growing potatoes.
Long house	A linear building providing accommodation for humans at one end and animals at the other.
Magnetic susceptibility measurement	Measurement of local distortions in the earth's magnetic field to indicate the presence of archaeological features.
Matrix	Mass of rock surrounding or adhering to things embedded in the earth.
Morphology	Study of the form of animals and plants; applied also to settlement studies.
Mysid	Shrimp-like marine animal living at the surface or middle of the sea.
Neolithic	The period of the first farming and permanent settlement.
Neonatal mortality	Death of the newly-born.
North Atlantic Drift	The North Atlantic ocean current produced by the prevailing wind.
Nucleated buildings	Buildings with a central core around which other parts are congregated.
Oestrus	Sexual heat of animals.
Optical alidade	Instrument used to plot the angles between survey stations and thus calculate the distance between them.
Orthostatic stones	Large stone slabs, set upright.
PCBs	Range of thermoplastic resins, widely used especially as moulding materials and films.
pH measurement	Measurement of the amount of alkalinity and acidity in a soil. The pH value of a soil is an indicator of the type of remains likely to survive in that soil.
Parturition	Act of bringing forth young.

Phosphate analysis	Analysis of the phosphate content of the soil to identify the former presence of bone occupation layers and the extent of settlement in archaeological sites.
Plane-table	A small drawing board mounted on a tripod and equipped with a sighting rule or alidade.
Phytoplankton	Drifting plant life in the upper waters of the sea.
Quadrat	A square area of ground marked off for study.
Radiocaesium	Contracted from radioactive caesium, a radioactive isotope recovered from the waste of nuclear reactors in nuclear power plant.
Resistivity meter	An instrument to measure the amount of resistance to the flow of electricity through soil and hence different dampness in the soil. This can indicate the presence of buried features.
Ridged cultivation	Cultivation method producing raised ridges and low furrows.
Rumen	The first division of the stomach used for storage of food before it is regurgitated, further masticated and re-swallowed.
Run-rig	A system of land allocation where tenants held their land in a number of rigs or strips scattered amongst those of their neighbours.
Rut	Periodic sexual excitement of male deer.
Sarking boards	Boards laid on rafters as a basis for roofing materials.
Scarp	Inner wall or slope.
Scree	Area of small, loose stones on a mountain slope.
Shieling	Temporary grazing area for animals, often with bothy accommodation.
Shinty	A game, similar to hockey, played with a ball and curved sticks.
Slype	A type of sledge used in agriculture to drag heavy loads.
Steatite	A kind of talc, soapstone.
Stell	A walled enclosure for animals.
Sward	An expanse covered in short grass.
Talan	A wall dividing humans from animals in a long house.

Theodolite	Surveying instrument for measuring horizontal and vertical angles by means of telescope.
Thermoluminescence dating	Laboratory examination of pottery to establish when it was fired, and gave off stored energy as light.
Transect	A line or belt of vegetation marked off for study.
Ungulate	Term used to cover a multitude of hooved grazing animals.
Vernacular building	Building in local style, not professionally designed.
Viscera	The interior organs of the body such as the heart and intestines.
Wall bed	Bed built within the thickness of a wall.
Wheelhouse	A circular type of house dating from the Iron Age. The interior is divided by radial stone piers projecting from the wall. The centre is left clear for a hearth.
Winnowing	Separating grain from chaff.
Zooplankton	Floating and drifting animal life in the seas and oceans.

St Kilda

List of Illustrations

St Kilda

Source of Illustrations

The publishers wish to thank the following who have kindly given permission to reproduce illustrations.

Peter Moore Photos, Front Cover.
John Clarke (Brick), Figure 4.
Sir John Dyke Acland, Figures 5, 16.
The George Washington Wilson Collection, Aberdeen University Library, Figures 9b, 18 .
Dr J Morton Boyd, CBE, Figure 10.
Royal Commission on the Ancient and Historical Monuments of Scotland, Crown Copyright Frontispiece, pvi and Figures 12, 25,26,27,28,29.
Alasdair Alpin MacGregor Collection, Scottish Ethnological Archive, National Museums of Scotland, Figure 20.
R C MacLeod of MacLeod Collection, School of Scottish Studies, University of Edinburgh, Figure 22.
The Society of Antiquaries of Scotland, Figure 23
Sue Scott, Figure 51
Frances Gulland, Figure 55
Jim Vaughn, Figure 62
All other illustrations are by the authors and Glasgow Museums photographers.

Numbering Systems

The numbering system for houses and cleitean follows that published in Stell and Harman, *Buildings of St Kilda,* 1988.

Archaelogical site numbers are those given by the excavators.

Index

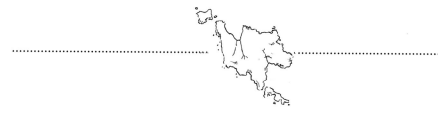

Page numbers in italics indicate illustrations

HMSO Bookshops
71 Lothian Road, Edinburgh EH3 9AZ
0131-228 4181 Fax 0131-229 2734
49 High Holborn, London WC1V 6HB
(counter service only)
0171-873 0011 Fax 0171-831 1326
68–69 Bull Street, Birmingham B4 6AD
0121-236 9696 Fax 0121-236 9699
33 Wine Street, Bristol BS1 2BQ
0117 9264306 Fax 0117 9294515
9-21 Princess Street, Manchester M60 8AS
0161-834 7201 Fax 0161-833 0634
16 Arthur Street, Belfast BT1 4GD
01232 238451 Fax 01232 235401
The HMSO Oriel Bookshop,
The Friary, Cardiff CF1 4AA
01222 395548 Fax 01222 384347

HMSO publications are available from:

HMSO Publications Centre
(Mail, fax and telephone orders only)
PO Box 276, London SW8 5DT
Telephone orders 0171-873 9090
General enquiries 0171-873 0011
(queuing system in operation for both numbers)
Fax orders 0171-873 8200

HMSO's Accredited Agents
(see Yellow Pages)

and through good booksellers

Printed in Scotland for HMSO by
CC No 13129 30C 6/95

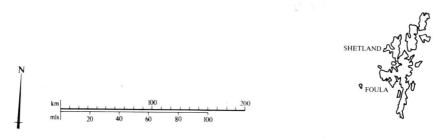

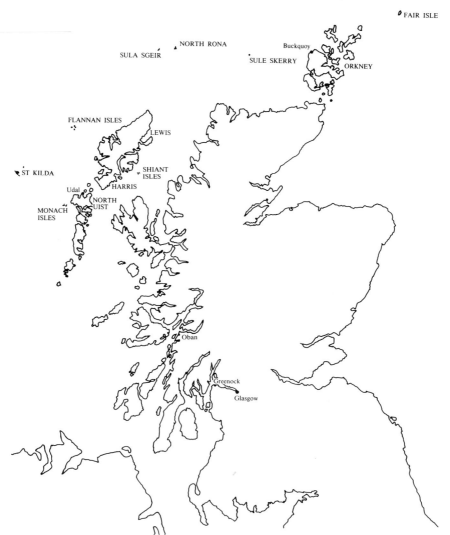

St Kilda in relation to mainland Scotland and the marrine environment.